MONEY TALKS

Ten Things I Wish My Parents Told Me About Finances

CHEENA R. ZOEGA

Printed in Australia.

ISBN 978-1-7635953-0-9

The material in this book is intended to be general in nature and does not consider your unique objectives, circumstances or needs into consideration. it should not be taken as financial advice. Readers should consider whether the information is appropriate and obtain independent professional advice where appropriate, before making such decision. To the maximum extent permitted by law, the author shall neither liability nor responsibility to any person or entity with respect to any perceived loss or damage caused, directly or indirectly, by the information contained in this book.

All events and scenarios in this book are based on my experience and were true and correct at the time of writing.

Contents

Chapter 1	First thing – set goals, have a plan, get it done	16
	What do YOU want?	16
	Map your journey – short, medium, long	18
	How to turn goals into reality?	19
	Early bird gets the worm	25
Chapter 2	Second thing – be a budgetista	31
	The baseline	33
	Progress check	36
	What the debt is that?	38
	4 simple tips to keep the budgetista on track	39
Chapter 3	Third thing – saving is the new black	42
	So how much $ do we have?	43
	How much $ do I need to save?	44
	8 money saving tips to get you started	46
Chapter 4	Fourth thing – avoid the 'pay later' temptation	50
	How do credit cards make their money?	52
	Buy now, pay later (BNPL)	53
Chapter 5	Fifth thing – have an insurance umbrella ready on a rainy day	57
	Life, TPD, income protection insurances	58
	Health insurance	60
	Home and contents insurance	61
	Car insurance	62
	Pet insurance	63

Chapter 6	Sixth thing – leave your mark with estate planning	65
	Will and testamentary trust	66
	Power of attorney	70
	Enduring power of guardianship	70
	Advanced Care Directive	71
	Superannuation	71
Chapter 7	Seventh thing – pay the right amount of tax: the Goldilocks principle	74
	How to pay the right amount of tax?	75
Chapter 8	Eighth thing – invest like a superwoman!	85
	Diversity is key	89
	Risk profile	90
	In it for the long haul	91
	Stocks	93
	Managed funds (including index funds)	101
	Exchange-traded funds (ETFs)	103
	Commodities	106
	Bonds	108
	Options	110
	Cryptocurrency	111
	NFTs	115
	Real estate	116
Chapter 9	Ninth thing – make your superannuation work for you	147
	Why super matters	149
	Getting super smart	150
Chapter 10	Tenth thing – a successful woman thrives with a winning team	163
	Start with yourself	164
	Your life partner	165
	Your network circle	166
	Your team of experts	167
	Last pearls of wisdom	172

To T.P.

My biggest cheerleader

whose words of encouragement make me beam with pride even when

I'm flushing with embarrassment

Preface

Once upon a time, there was a beautiful princess stuck in a castle, waiting for a handsome and brave prince to rescue her. She didn't know who this hero was or when he would come, but she hoped her knight would show up soon because she didn't know how she would escape the castle by herself. Day after day, she waited. One day, lo-and-behold, the prince arrived at her doorstep after slaying some dragons and defeating some villains. They fell in love and lived happily ever after.

Sigh.

Even though this scenario is totally unlikely to happen in real life, it's a fictitious narrative that still pervades many of the romance novels we read or romantic movies and K-dramas we watch. But this outdated rhetoric sits uneasily with me as a financially independent woman in the 21st century.

Not that long ago, a woman was expected to give up her education or career when she married, so she could take care of the family while her husband pursued his career. Then somehow she would find herself in a pickle when they divorced, or he had a midlife crisis, and she had no employable skills, children in tow and no means to live her previous comfortable life. Is the scenario above an old-fashioned and overused trope then? Absolutely. And have we all heard similar stories about women finding themselves in a tough spot financially? Definitely.

You, and only you, are responsible and accountable for setting yourself up for financial success. Nobody can do that for you. But the fact that you have picked up this book shows you are seeking knowledge and ways to set up your kick-ass independent future. Good on you! Some of us may have a partner with whom we can share financial and emotional burdens. Some of us are happily single and living a full, busy life. Wherever you are at in your life's journey, it is important to think about the future and the day you might want to put your feet up and enjoy a well-deserved 'retirement' and the many milestones you achieved along the way.

In a world where information is readily available at our fingertips, your everyday smartphone contains access to more knowledge and has more digital processing power than a room-sized super-computer 60 years ago. It's really up to us how we harness this infinite knowledge source. We've all been tempted to spend hours scrolling through social media and looking at viral videos. But we also have this great opportunity to use our precious time on more meaningful endeavours, like building our future.

There is so much information out there – where do we even start?

That's the aim of this book – to be a starting point. I want to share with you the 10 things I wish my parents taught me about finances to set me on my merry path. I want this book to inspire you with hope for your financial future (however that looks like to you), to light the path ahead as you take steps in that direction and get started on your journey of financial empowerment.

Introduction – financial basics every savvy woman should know

My parents were first-generation immigrants. They both grew up during the Chinese cultural revolution and endured more hardship than I can imagine; the stories they have shared are mind-boggling. When I was 10 years old, they left their jobs as medical doctors and came to New Zealand – a very different culture from the one they were used to. With limited language skills, resources and social support, they worked in menial jobs to get by. After spending their last thousand dollars on an extremely run-down car, it promptly got stolen five weeks from the day my dad told us he'd discovered any old car key could open the driver door. Despite the many challenges they faced, they worked extremely hard and tried to provide the best they could so we could survive in this new country. They managed to make themselves a home and build a new life.

There was a lot of expectation from my new-immigrant parents when I was growing up. At the top of the list was to study hard and get good grades, so that you could get a secure job with a steady income. You would then work your way up the corporate ladder and become the epitome of success. There wasn't a lot of talk of following your dreams, how to get a passive income and finding your *ikigai* (life purpose) – these ideas were a luxury we didn't think about.

The subjects we studied at school provided us with a foundational knowledge of core academic concepts. The education system prioritised academic success and prepared us for traditional future pursuits. While I found the value of x more times than I care to remember during maths classes, I felt my education missed the very thing I needed the most: practical skills for everyday life.

After leaving school, and especially when we first leave home, we are pushed out into the 'real' world. It's like being handed the keys to a car without actually knowing how to drive. Suddenly we are expected to manage everything ourselves. Simple, yet important things like finding a place to live, cooking and managing money can feel overwhelming.

I certainly wish I was more prepared for these practical things, especially around finances. I remember when the banks offered interest-free overdrafts while I was a university student. It took me years to pay that loan back. After graduation, I entered the workforce with stars in my eyes. It wasn't long before I realised it wasn't what I thought it would be. I thought I would be working on cutting-edge ideas, collaborating with enthusiastic, like-minded individuals and changing the world for the better. Before I knew it, I was disillusioned with the daily grind, office politics and working long hours for someone else.

I'm sure you, like me, have heard enough mentions of the book *Rich Dad, Poor Dad* to know that the path to financial freedom can't be answered by the conventional 'get a good job' script we were given. But I just couldn't figure out what the path was, if not a 'good job'. Neither school nor conversations around the dinner table address these gaps.

When you are a standard PAYG worker, you're selling hours. If you don't work those hours, then you don't get paid. My parents taught me the importance of saving. But you can only save a certain amount per year, so doesn't that mean you just have to keep on working until you reach retirement age? Then, finally, you get to enjoy some well-deserved rest and do all the things you've been wanting to do all your life ... assuming you're still healthy and able-bodied enough, right?

I knew I had to do something different. I knew I had to get educated in finances. I knew I needed to be financially smarter so that I could have the freedom to do whatever I wanted but I had no idea where to start. I didn't even know how to answer the questions that came up like *'How do I pay just the right amount of taxes?', 'How does the Medicare levy impact on my earning?'* and *'What do I invest my money in?'*

Financial freedom can only start with financial literacy. Financial literacy is not just for those who work in the financial industry. It is for all of us. It helps us to make decisions about how we earn, spend and save money, how to invest our hard-earned dollars and our retirement. Nobody is born with it, it is learnt. And anyone can learn it, but the earlier you start, the more practice you get, the better you get at handling money and more financially confident you become. It's hard to become a concert pianist if you only read and memorise the notes. It requires dedicated practice, over and over again.

Historically, men have held the role of breadwinner and decision maker, which afforded them greater financial freedom and general rights. As more and more women joined the labour market throughout the 1900s, becoming increasingly visible in working life, our access to paid work has improved, but the social hangovers of those times still present a major obstacle to financial independence and equity. From limited education and unequal employment opportunities to societal and cultural expectations, the odds have been stacked against us. So it is of little surprise that women tend to feel less capable in their financial knowledge and understanding than men.

If we got into a time machine, you would see that women's financial rights have been like a tug of war between moving forward and slipping back. In ancient Egypt, women had many of the same financial rights as men. We could make business deals, sign contracts, and own property and assets. Not all women used these rights because of social stigma.

Under the law of coverture in medieval England, husbands and wives were seen as one financial entity, and a married woman's legal existence was merged with her husband's. If you ran a business, then all the profit and assets belonged to your husband. If you had inherited property, then that automatically became your husband's. If you wanted to enter into a legal contract, you need your husband's consent and signature. If you were involved in legal issues, then your husband would make decisions on your behalf as your representative.

Fast forward to the 20th century – the 1960s marked the first time that Australian women didn't have to quit their jobs in the public service once they were married (and women were finally allowed to drink in a public bar!). However, it wasn't until the 1970s that a woman could secure a loan without requiring a male guarantor. The situation wasn't exactly better in other parts of the world; in the United States, it was still legal to discriminate against pregnant women until 1978, so your employer was legally allowed to fire you if you became pregnant before this time. I know that's some time ago, but it's still too close to today's date for my comfort.

No wonder it is difficult for women to feel secure in their financial independence when these types of gender inequalities exist. There have been substantial strides made since then and we have come a long way. Most of us would be outraged by not being able to have our names on something that belongs to us, and we no longer need to concern ourselves about not being able to open our own bank account.

We need to take advantage of these rights and use them to their full potential. After all, we want to run the world! So it is more important than ever for us to get our financial futures sorted. And why is that?

Today, even though 47% of the global workforce is female (that number is 61%[1] in Australia), we still earn an average of 22.8%[2] less than our male counterparts. So if you work a 40-hour week, you are working just over 9 hours in that week for free. The gender pay gap only gets scarier if you are a woman of colour.

47%	61%	23%
Global workforce	Australian workforce	Earn 23% less than males

There are many factors which may contribute towards why women earn less. Perhaps we gravitate towards jobs that require more flexibility, or jobs that offer more work–life balance, or we take more time out of the workforce to care for family. Whatever the reason, it means we have less money to save, invest, pay off debt or invest in our careers or businesses. The focus of this book is not to tell you to 'lean in' and get your seat at the table, although you are absolutely entitled to that seat ... or to own the damn building if you want to.

We are also likely to live longer than men. According to the World Health Organization, women have a life expectancy of around five years longer. In Australia, the average life expectancy is around 85 years of age for a female.[3] If we use 67 as the retirement age, that is 18 years where you hopefully won't have to work and can continue having a comfortable lifestyle. Unfortunately, this is not the case for many women in Australia. Workplace Gender Equality Agency research[4] shows that elderly women were more likely than men to re-enter the workforce and twice as likely to sell their house after retirement due to financial constraints.

This should not happen.

If the thought of working until 67 fills you with dread and you can't see yourself working until the retirement age, then you need to have a good grasp on your financial situation. Unless you're an heir to an unlimited fortune or have access to a money tree, understanding financial basics is essential. In this book, I am going to teach them to you.

Knowledge is power. But knowledge is only powerful if you use it. By taking practical steps to use what you know, you can take control, establish financial independence and achieve financial security. This will help to give you peace of mind and makes sure that you are well prepared for whatever life throws your way.

You're the CEO, COO and CFO of your money. You are the ultimate decision-maker, master strategist and architect of your financial future – so build something fills you with pride and joy. I hope this book becomes one of your favourite topics to discuss and spark conversations around the dinner table – may it pique your curiosity and inspire you to take action.

First thing – set goals, have a plan, get it done

What do YOU want?

First things first, there's a reason why you picked up this book. You are curious, you want to know more about finances, money and how to set up your financial future. But ... why?

All too often, I hear the words 'financial freedom' or 'financial independence'. But what does this mean for you personally?

- Is it to be able to retire comfortably?
- Is it to have a certain amount of money in the bank?
- Is it to live well on a single income with a growing family?
- Is it to travel the world and never have to worry about work?

Whatever drives you, that's your North Star. Your guiding light. The 'why' to your 'what'. Otherwise, how can you budget if you don't know what you're trying to do with that money? How would you know you have saved enough if you don't know what you're saving for and how much you need? How would you know if you are at your destination if you never set an end point?

I personally think the most important, rewarding thing to think about is why you're doing it and what you're looking to do. It's not about money or finances, it's about giving meaning to your dreams. It will help you to make choices that align with your aspirations and stay focused when things get tough. Consider the following questions:

- Why are you thinking about your financial future?
- What do you actually want to achieve?
- What is important and why is this important to you?

For me, it is to achieve financial independence. My definition of financial independence isn't driving a fancy car or living in a swanky house; it means having the choice and control over how I live. It means if I work, then it's because I want to not because I have to. It means going on holidays when I want, so I can experience different cultures and eat amazing local food. It means having enough spare time to spend quality time with family and friends, without worrying about paying the bills.

Despite how important it is, goal setting is difficult. I have definitely spent a big chunk of my days not thinking about my financial future, and just researching topics or investing in assets when the mood would strike. It was only when I really thought about what I wanted to achieve and why, the pathway became clearer. That's also when I became more determined and able to act faster. This is the power of your North Star.

Map your journey – short, medium, long

It is said that most people underestimate how much they can achieve in a year and overestimate what they can do in a day. This certainly rings true for me – I used to always have too many items on my to-do list and would get annoyed when I only manage to cross half of it off by the end of the day.

I like to think of setting goals as being like a road trip.

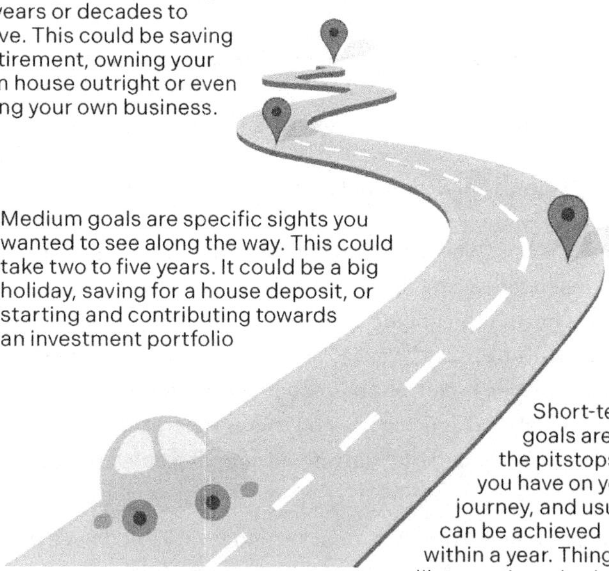

These goals are forming the map of your financial future – keeping you on track and providing direction as to where you need to go.

Everyone has different goals and different circumstances, so naturally the roads to get to wherever we are heading are going to look different.

Even if you have similar goals to someone else, they might be driving a Ferrari and you might be on a bicycle, so it's not fair to compare. Besides, you've got to keep your eyes on the road!

> Everyone is on their own journey, so use your energy to focus on your own and do not compare it to someone else's.

How to turn goals into reality?

One of the reasons why setting goals is so powerful is that you then have an action plan to work towards. Only when you start executing the plan will things really get moving. The earlier you get things moving, the bigger the impact will be.

Are they SMART?

The most effective way of setting goals is using the SMART principle. This can be applied to all of the goal setting you are doing, no matter the timeline or the type of goals. I like to use it whenever I can.

Quite a few years ago, I started a health and fitness routine because I wanted to take better care of my body. I became obsessed with the idea of running a marathon. Perhaps it was because I was getting bombarded with articles about how running releases endorphins and I kept seeing svelte people clad in activewear sprinting past when I was strolling leisurely through a park. They made it look so easy. I wanted to experience this runner's high too!

I had never run more than a couple of times around the block at that point, so I thought starting with the goal of a half-marathon was more sensible than a full-fledged marathon. I was not a natural runner and certainly didn't have a runner's physique. I had my work cut out for me but I was determined. This is where SMART goals come in. This is what I used:

Specific

I want to complete the Melbourne half-marathon and run the entire way.

Measurable

I want to run 21 km and complete the race in under 2 hours (with a secret stretch goal of 1:45 hours)

Achievable

I will join a running club, follow the recommended training plan and enter shorter races prior to the half-marathon as preparation.

Relevant

I am determined to achieve this because this aligns with my personal fitness goals. Running will help with my physical and mental wellbeing. I am willing to put in the time and effort to make sure I have every chance of completing the race.

Time-bound

I will register for the tickets three months before the race and I will enter the half-marathon race in October.

And you know what, I did it! I must admit I was quite chuffed with myself. The official time showed I was 27 seconds over my stretch goal. It just goes to show – hard work, discipline and a bit of self-belief will get you to the finish line.

SMART goals are a great way to keep you on track and increase your chances of achieving these goals.[5] It is important to set goals for different timelines – short, medium or long term. This keeps them real and makes it easier to stay motivated and engaged, you might as well enjoy the ride!

When you have SMART goals, you spend time thinking about how you will get there and plan accordingly, which gives you time to pivot and finesse your actions to reach your goals. Think about the times when you're learning a new skill or hobby; the more you focus on it and the more time you spend doing it, the better you get.

Stretch yourself

I'm a big fan of stretch goals – something that is just a little out of reach but not completely. A 2002 analysis reviewing research spanning 35 years showed the goal needs to be challenging enough for you to make a connection to it, and you need to have a connection to move ahead.[6] If the goal is too easy, you will just get bored. And if it is completely out of reach, you're setting yourself up to fail before you even start. You want to make sure you set yourself up for success. Have you ever put yourself on a super strict diet, slipped and had a little treat, then suddenly you've eaten the whole bag of chips and abandoned the diet altogether? Moral of the story? Create realistic stretch goals.

Let's say you are a great jewellery designer and have been creating amazing pieces for family and friends. You have been playing around with the idea of spending more time doing this instead of your normal day job. Perhaps a stretch goal could look like this – within the next two years, I will launch and grow my own successful business. I will sell my jewellery through market stalls and online shops. My target profit margin is 40% or higher and I will earn a 5-figure ($50,000) income through this business by the end of the second year.

Break it down

Another way to achieve those big goals is to trick your own mind, a.k.a. take advantage of your brain's intrinsic reward pathway: the dopamine system.

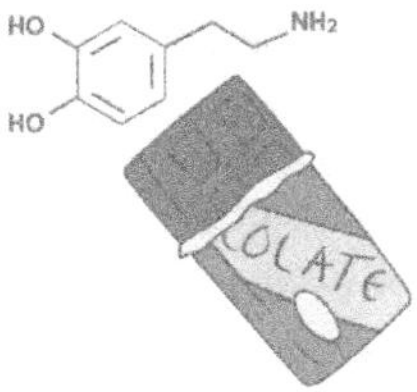

When we get something we want, we release a feel-good neurotransmitter called dopamine. A 2019 study in *Nature* mentioned when we set goals and when we're close to accomplishing those goals, we get a hit of dopamine.[7] Dopamine is addictive! Did you know we also get a hit when we eat chocolate? This is one of the reasons why we love chocolate so much.

If we can break those big or long-term goals into smaller ones, achieving bite-sized goals as we go, dopamine is going to help keep you motivated. Hits of dopamine are the quintessential snacks you need on your road trip of success.

Write it down

Studies have suggested writing goals down regularly can increase the chances of them happening. A hefty 42% increase in fact.[8] This helps to cement the goals in our heads and makes them tangible and therefore more actionable.

My husband and I have an annual wine and cheese night at the start of the year. We sit down with a piece of paper (yes, old school) and reflect back on the year that was, and set some goals for the year ahead, and we compare how we're tracking against our 5, 10, 20-year goals. We have our own personal goals and combined ones together.

We use this as a chance to celebrate our wins and get a hit of dopamine. Or is it from the wine and cheese? Either way, it works! Celebrating milestones remind you that you have achieved so much in the last 12 months. It's working so well that we have started doing it every few months. It is too easy if you are constantly striving or working hard towards your

North Star goals to forget to acknowledge your accomplishments. Taking a moment to savour the satisfaction of an achievement helps to fuel your motivation further.

Having an allocated time set to do this every year (or more often) reminds you of what great things you have done, keeps you accountable and allows you to anticipate the great things instore for you in the year ahead. You get to decide what you will be celebrating next year. How exciting is that?!

Pivot if you need to

We can't always plan for everything. Sometimes there are road closures or unexpected roadblocks along the way. It's important to recognise that it is okay to pivot when the reasons are valid, and remember to be kind to yourself. There's no perfect way to get somewhere, so got to keep your eye on the bigger picture!

Let's say that you're saving up for a house deposit, but then your personal circumstances change. You might have an unexpected but welcomed pregnancy, or you get caught up in company redundancies, and it might be necessary to pivot and adjust your goals. Maybe it will take you six months longer. The important thing is that you get back on track. It's about working towards your plans and know where you are going, but being flexible enough to be able to change your path and always seek and be open to new opportunities.

Take action

Once you have the initial goal setting and planning done, you can start taking action towards achieving your goals. This is where the fun really begins!

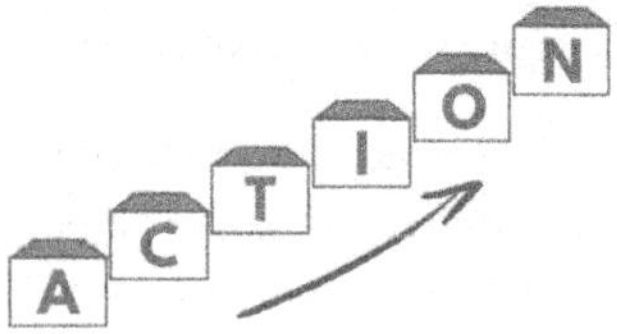

Taking action is like shifting your car's gear to drive and where rubber meets the road. You are no longer just thinking about it, you're doing it. Look at you go!

You might have to change specific goals as life gives you lemons or adapt bigger goals if your current ones are too easy. As long as you are moving, you are taking steps towards achieving your goals. So just do something. Whether it's a baby step or a giant leap, life is often a sequence of small actions over time.

Goal setting, planning and taking action are proactive steps you are taking. But what's the point in gaining knowledge and doing all the planning if you don't do anything with it? Doing nothing is also a choice. One that we should be aware we are making.

The rest of this book gives ideas and prompts for different parts of your financial life. Every time you act, it brings you a little closer to your goals and that beautiful future you have imagined for yourself as it begins to take shape. You are building it one action at a time.

Early bird gets the worm

One of my long-term goals is an early retirement, well ... earlier than the age of 67 anyway. Having this as my North Star goal has allowed me to plan out different actions to take in the short and medium term. I have made a lot of mistakes along the way, but I'm learning and improving as I go.

We have already talked about how women earn less and live longer. This means setting specific financial goals is super important to make sure there is a game plan in place.

Let's take a look at what the government will be providing for us at the average age of retirement. The maximum basic rate is $882.20 for a single person or $1330 for a couple in a fortnight (as of October 2021). That's the amount allocated *per fortnight*...

If you adore your career and never want to retire, will your income support the lifestyle you want? If you are like me and want to retire early, how much do you actually need? Of course, the average amount a person needs for retirement is going to be different. There are a lot of variables – for example:

- At what age are you planning to retire?
- What kind of lifestyle are you planning to have?
- What kind of expenses are you likely to incur as a result?
- How long do you think you will live?
- What is the likely income you will receive?

These are just some questions to consider when you're thinking about your long-term retirement goals. By using your goals as the guide, it will help you to determine your plan. Either way, if we go back to the numbers we just saw, it's unlikely the basic rate is going to allow you to retire comfortably.

Tip – when you are doing this exercise, don't forget to add in % increase per year to allow for the increase in living costs. And be honest with your calculations – if your current expenses are $20,000 per year, it may not be feasible to suddenly aim for $100,000 year in your retirement.

No matter what, it is never too early to plan for your long-term future. As the Chinese proverb says, 'The best time to plant a tree was 20 years ago. The second-best time is now.' The future you will thank the present-day you. I have never met a person who wished they started investing or thinking about their personal finances later. It's almost always, 'Oh, I wish I started earlier.' In fact, the earlier you start planning, the better. One of the reasons for this is the power of *compounding*. If you're not excited about this concept, then get ready ... you definitely will be soon!

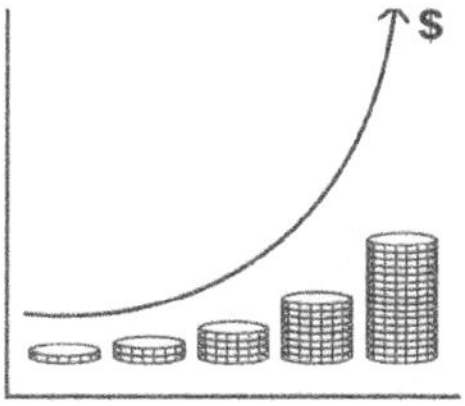

Let's look at an example – Jo, Zara and Elie are good friends. They each have different money styles and different lives, but they all want to retire at the age of 67. They each made an equal contribution of $200,000 over the years to an interest-earning account with a 5% return. However, they all started contributing at different ages: Jo started early at 25, Zara at 35 and Elie at 45. Let's take a look at how compounding affects the outcome.

Jo started at 25 years old

Total contribution
$200,000

Annual contribution
$5,000 per year

Total accumulated at 67 years old (with 5% average return per year

$750,715

Zara started at 35 years old

Total contribution
$200,000

Annual contribution
$6,667 per year

Total accumulated at 67 years old (with 5% average return per year

$560,475

Even though Jo put in the least amount each year compared to her friends, she has significantly more money at age 67. Because it's not just $5000 she invests every year, it's also the additional interest that gets compounded. This trend continues, with each year's amount building upon the previous year, earning interest on the interest.

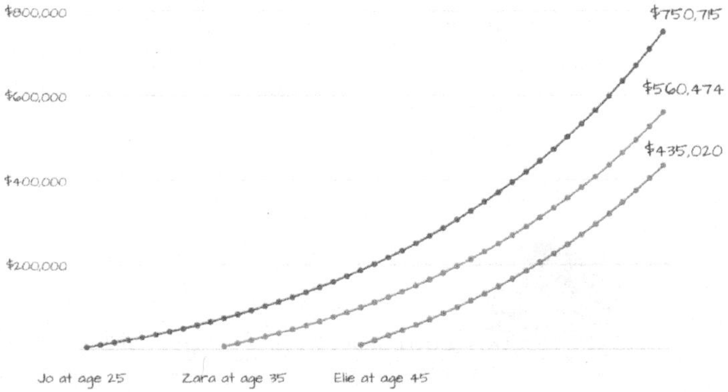

This is the power of compounding. The earlier you start, the more time your money has to grow, and the more you will have.

But remember this is also the same for your debts. There will be more on that in a later chapter.

TAKE CHARGE

Sit down somewhere without distractions. It could be just you or you and someone important in your life.

Grab a pen and paper. Or if you want to get super creative, then do it vision-board style with markers and scrapbooks.

Write a list of all the goals you have – everything you want to achieve – and don't forget to apply the SMART principles. It could be your own personal goals, or couple or family goals. Write down as many as you can – ideally at least two of each – short term, medium term and long term.

This is SUPER exciting because you are looking at your dreams for your future, so make it fun! Maybe you could do it with a glass of your favourite wine (or tea), and with some delicious dinner or snacks. Whatever floats your boat.

TAKE CHARGE

Once you have written your goals down, keep them somewhere handy. These are your dreams for the future, so why not put them somewhere visible as a constant reminder of what you're working towards?

Lastly, don't forget to set a recurring reminder for you to check your progress against your goals, review them further and set new goals.

Second thing – be a budgetista

Once you have set your goals, the wheels are now in motion in creating an action plan to get you there. But you need to know your starting point – where are you right now?

The next step is to take control of your money situation – you have to know what you've got. You need to know what's coming in and what's going out. Without a good handle on your current incomings and outgoings, how would you know if you're on track? In order to work towards your goal and build your financial future, your 'in' needs to be more than your 'out'. It seems so simple right?

Reality tells us otherwise.

Australia is one of the wealthiest countries in the world. But it seems even in this sunny land of riches, financial stress has found its way into the lives of many working Australian women. The numbers don't lie.

In 2020, 19% of women were facing moderate or severe financial stress, and that number has jumped to 27% in just two years.[9] That is over a quarter of working women. This is a sobering number.

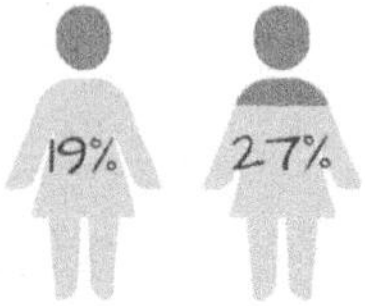

In taking control of your financial situation, knowing where you are right now gives you a baseline to start from. It can help you with where to focus, guide you on your spending, and most importantly – make sure that your money balance is working for you. This is where a budget comes in. Having a budget will form your financial foundation.

I was very 'money-lazy' in my younger years, just relying on the fact I spent less than I earned. I never checked my bank balance and thought I lived rather frugally. It wasn't until my debit card got declined for a $1 purchase, that I took note and started to take budgeting seriously. It was a wakeup call to remind me I wasn't as good with money as I thought.

When I first started this exercise, I took three simple steps:

1. I asked, 'Where do I want to go?' and set some goals (we discussed this in the first chapter).

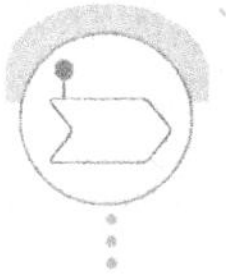

2. I set the baseline by looking at where I am today.

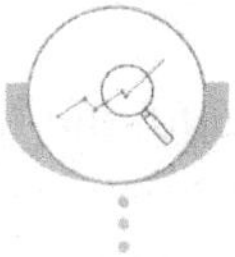

3. I considered how I was tracking – i.e. I kept tabs of my money.

The baseline

Everyone does it differently, but using a spreadsheet really worked for me. It can be a super simple way to keep track of your incomings and outgoings.

Your incoming can include all your sources of income, e.g:

- income from your job or your own business
- income from your side hustles
- income from any investments, such as dividends.

Your outgoings can include all of your spending, e.g:

- rent or mortgage repayments
- bills – water, rates, electricity, gas, phone and internet
- entertainment – dining out, evening activities etc
- insurances – health, car, life etc
- transport – fuel, public transport
- food and groceries.

Income	Weekly/monthly	Outgoings	Weekly/monthly
Salary		Rent/mortgage	
Bonus		Electricity/gas	
Side hustles		House repair and maintenance (cleaning, pest, garden)	
Investments		Rates and levies (council, water, strata)	
Miscellaneous		Phone/internet	
		Food (groceries, deliveries)	
		Household expenses (cleaning, laundry)	
		Insurance (health, home and content, car, life, pet)	
		Transport (car, tolls, public transport, petrol)	
		Entertainment (gifts, subscriptions, memberships, eating out)	

		Health (medical expenses, gym membership, etc)	
		Education (fees, books)	
		Loan payments (credit card, personal loans, student loans)	
		Family care (childcare fees, elderly care, pet care)	
		Clothing and beauty	
		Travel (holiday expenses)	
		Charity donations	
Total income		Total outgoings	
		Miscellaneous	
		Income – outgoings =	$ left over
			If there's nothing left over, then your budget needs to change.

Track this for a few months to give you an idea of your spending habits. Sometimes this can be quite a confronting exercise, but it's a very important one.

When I did this exercise, it really helped me to prioritise which expenses were the most important and which weren't. I was genuinely quite shocked at how much money I spent on entertainment and dining out. It certainly made me think twice about whether I should buy a cocktail on a Wednesday night.

Progress check

Now you have an idea of what's coming in and what's going out, it's time to move onto how you're tracking.

Even though we may have the best intentions, not many of us are going to update a spreadsheet every single week or month for long. To the diligent unicorns out there, I salute you! For the rest of us, perhaps a more manageable way to keep a budget is to divide up your income. There are many ways to slice up the pie. But for the sake of ease, there are three big slices you could consider, the size of which depends on your unique circumstances.

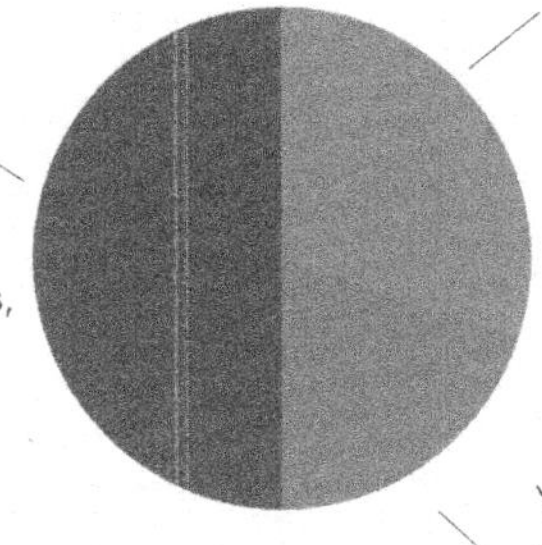

Some debts are 'good' debts. That's usually debts used to buy assets that are going to generate income or grow in value over time – e.g. borrowing money to buy investments. Even though you are borrowing money, it is in the hope your investment will grow in value and generate more gains than the money you put in.

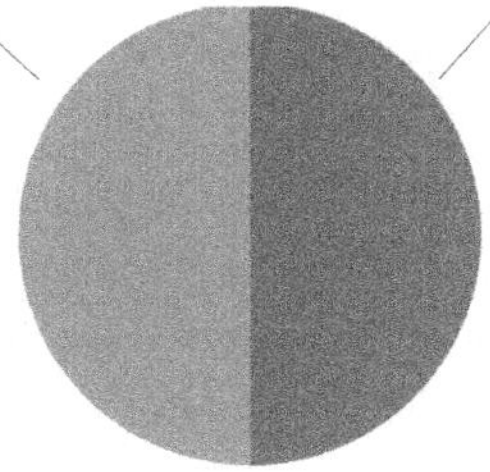

Some debts are 'bad' debts. That's any debts with high interest rates, depreciating assets or when you have borrowed money for unnecessary purchases – e.g. borrowing money for a flashy car or excessive shopping. Sure, you might look good, but there is no further growth from the money you spent.

However big you want each of these slices to be, it's important you put at least 20% towards your rainy day / savings fund. Some people like to divide this even further and be really specific – x% for a house deposit and x% for extra payments towards your superannuation. Do what is the best for you. I have friends who have set up separate bank accounts for each of these because it's easier to keep track. If this is something you are going to do, don't forget to read the fine print to make sure you're not charged a monthly fee – after all, you don't want any pesky fees eating away at your money.

The pie slices can sometimes look quite different for people. Some of you may have heard of the FIRE movement. FIRE stands for 'Financial Independence, Retire Early'. The goal, as the name suggest, is to gain financial independence and retire early. The key themes behind FIRE are to save as much money as you can, invest well and live frugally. FIRE followers aim to save and invest up to 70% of their income. That's a big piece of pie. Imagine the goal setting, detailed planning and discipline of these followers!

For the rest of us mere mortals, pie slices could change at different times too, depending on our priorities. The important thing is to be diligent and methodical with how you divide up your money. The more you can place in your rainy day / savings fund, the more money you will have to invest! More on this in Chapter 8.

What the debt is that?

I want to call out debt here. Managing your debt is essential when it comes to budgeting. I'm talking here about credit cards, mortgages, student loans, car loans etc. Of course, not all debts are created equal and it would be worthwhile for you to carefully consider the type of debt you have and its impact on your financial future.

Since these types of debt are not the same, it may be a good idea to prioritise them differently. Having bad debts is like taking a walk with a weighted vest. The heaviest weights are the ones with high interest. It can be a heavy burden holding you back and making every step more difficult in your financial life. When it comes to managing your debt, it may make more sense to tackle the 'bad' debts first because these are the weights that make walking more difficult. Get rid of them so you can move faster and a lot more freely. Good debts are like planting seeds for the future. You have to put up the initial investment of buying quality seeds and take good care of them with nutrients and water, but you do so in the hopes of reaping the rewards at harvest time.

If you have debts you're dealing with, it can feel a bit scary. When I had the overdraft during my university days, the amount I owed seemed daunting – after all, I was a university student whose staple diet was 2-minute noodles and canned tuna. I dealt with the loan by burying my head in the sand and avoided thinking about it at all. No wonder it took me so long to pay it back!

If you're in need of a financial counsellor, contact the National Debt Helpline at 1800 007 007. This is a free hotline for those with financial difficulties. The website National Debt Helpline also has more resources to help.

4 simple tips to keep the budgetista on track

Quick tip

Here are some helpful budgeting tips and tricks I picked up along the way:

1. Pay off your bad debt first.

   Remember the compounding we talked about before? Debt is the same and can quickly build up, so try to get rid of it as quickly as possible.

   Two common ways to attack debt: the *avalanche* method and the *snowball* method.

   The avalanche prioritises high interest debts while snowball focuses on the smallest debt first. Avalanche advocates that by paying off the high interest first, you can save more money in the long run because you can minimise the amount of interest you are paying and pay off the debts more quickly. Snowball advocates by paying off the smaller debts first, you get a sense of accomplishment and this gives you a motivation boost to keep on moving forward and tackling the bigger debts.

   Choose the method that suits you best. If you need motivation to get started, the snowball approach might be a good option. If you just want to tackle it head on, avalanche might be the best option for you, costing you less money and time.

2. Automate your income into different funds/accounts.

   Let's remove the temptation of dipping into your essentials fund when it probably should be coming out of your splurge fund. By automatically allocating money into separate accounts, especially your savings fund, it makes it just a little harder to do. It's a bit like 'out of sight, out of mind'. If you don't see it, it becomes harder to spend it!

3. Categorise your spending.

   Analyse your spending patterns and categorise into: 'must have', 'nice to have' and 'want to have'. For example, rent is a must have. This is going to help you take a good look at your expenses so you can better prioritise and identify areas you can cut back on if you need to.

4. Use cash as much possible.

   Instead of using a card, use cash. There have been several studies to show that people tend to spend less when they use cash. When using a card, people tend to underestimate the amount they are spending and spend more overall. There's even a study that shows people enjoy their purchases more when they use cash.[10]

   If using cash is a major nuisance, then maybe try to put a spending cap on your card and track your expenses diligently throughout the day/week/month (not just once at the end of the month). The intent is to prevent mindless tapping for your purchases and make you more conscious of your spending habits.

5. Stay consistent, review and adjust when you need to.

   It's all about forming good money habits. Aiming for your specific goals will help with the discipline you need to stick to your budget. Set percentages for those pie slices to help you keep on track. If you are prone to impulse buy, having good habits and sticking to your budget will help with your financial discipline. You don't stay the same person forever, so it doesn't make sense to have the same budget forever. If your circumstances change, it's a good idea to review your budget. Why not make it into a regular exercise? After all, it has to work for you!

TAKE CHARGE

What are three things you will action this week?

Here are some suggestions:

Download a budget app or start your own spreadsheet. Challenge yourself to do it for at least a month to form your own baseline. If you have a partner, this could be a good exercise to do together.

If you know your outgoings are consistently larger than your income, go over your spending and identify areas where you can make some changes.

Have a serious money and budget discussion with a trusted friend, partner or family member. You might be surprised to find discussing things and having some support is just the motivation you need to keep you accountable.

Third thing – saving is the new black

Budgeting and saving often go hand in hand. My parents taught me the importance of saving, but I have also learnt excessive saving with a scarcity mindset can lead to a person missing out on enjoying today. Finding a balance between saving for the future and enjoying life today is important. Hopefully you don't have to touch your rainy day fund, but it's good to be ready. Let's face it, it's not about the money; it's about the peace of mind in knowing that you will be okay if something does happen.

This is why I call bullsh*t on the idea that money can't buy you happiness. It definitely doesn't guarantee happiness or life fulfilment like being in good health or having great relationships does, but it is pretty fundamental. Having money takes care of your most basic needs such as shelter, clothing and food. Not having to worry about essential needs removes stress and provides the stability for you to live your life, have experiences and pursue life goals.

Financial stress has a negative effect on mental wellbeing. People dealing with financial stress are four times more likely to experience mental distress than those who are not.[11] Anxiety, depression and behaviours or thoughts related to suicide are more common in people facing financial hardship.

Out of the 38 wealthiest countries in the OECD, Australia has the 15th highest poverty rate according to the Australian Council of Social Service.[12] From a dollar perspective, the poverty line is at $489 a week for a single adult and $1027 a week for a family including two kids.[13] This is a hugely troubling statistic.

So how much $ do we have?

According to finder.com.au, in 2024, the average Australian has $37,915 in savings and saves $729 each month.

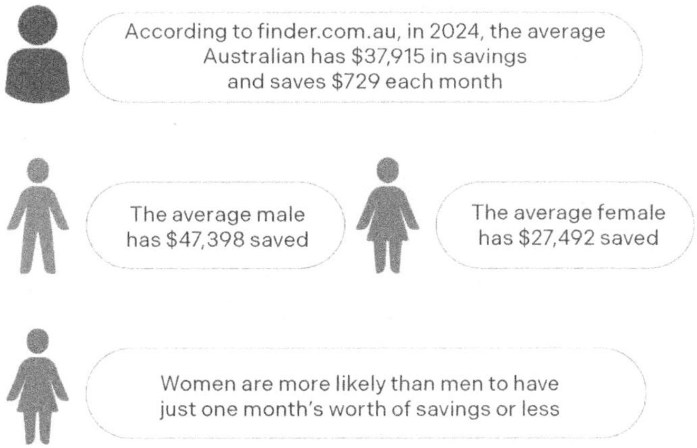

The difference in savings between males and females is particularly prominent among Millennials – with men having 68% more savings than females, followed by Gen X with 62%, and Gen Z at 53%.

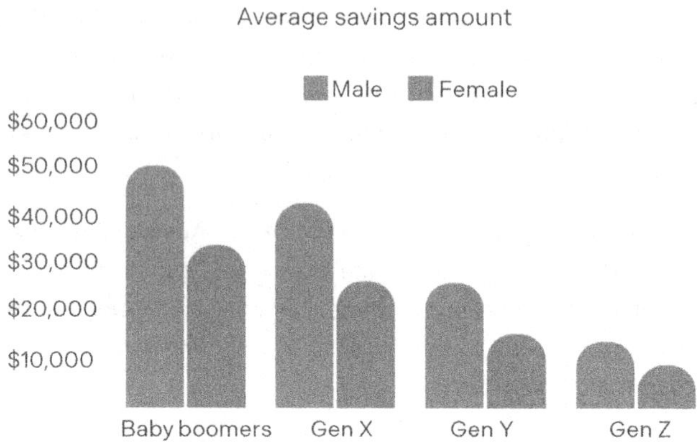

Figure 1: *source – Finder Consumer Sentiment Tracker, Jul 21–Jun 22*

While these may just sound like numbers, they do have serious repercussions around how a person lives and what this means for our everyday lives – financially, mentally and physically.

How much $ do I need to save?

How much money should you be saving? What's the right amount? My numbers became clear after I set my goals and budget. But for a 'rainy day' fund, there are really no hard and fast rules. Many financial planners recommend having enough savings to cover three to nine months' worth of expenses should things go south for you. I find this to be a rather large range to choose from. Personally, I use six months as my buffer as that's the sweet spot based on my personal experience with expenses and the length of time it takes to get a good alternative source of income.

Eighth thing – invest like a superwoman!

It doesn't matter if you're working part time or full time, or you're a business owner, investing is important. It is important for your long-term financial goals. I'm sure you can think of many reasons why it's important already, but here's a few to get you warmed up:

- To become financially independent, and have extra income to supplement and potentially takeover your primary income source
- To build wealth through passive income and capital growth, and have your money grow and multiply creating financial security for you and your loved ones
- To shape your own legacy, and create generational wealth for your loved ones.

Having all your cash sitting in your bank account is not a wise investment choice. Yes, having a rainy-day fund is a necessity, but when you have excess, then it's time to kick into high gear and make that excess

You can use this as a guide but use your own judgement to decide what is relevant for you. Factors like what costs you can cut back on and how quickly you can supplement your income will help you determine what's adequate for you. It's really about having enough of a safety net to help to bridge the gap when things get tough. This safety net provides some comfort and peace of mind if you do need it. I'm sure we can all agree that we don't need the extra mental stress of falling into debt.

When it comes to saving, being consistent is important. When you're putting aside a portion every week or fortnight or month, you're doing more than just putting money into your savings. You are forming a financial habit. This is even more important than how much money you started with. These habits will help you stick with your financial goals.

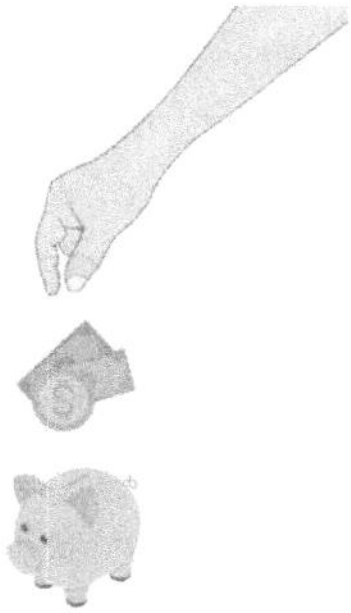

A friend of mine used to be a terrible saver, or rather, had no savings at all. They earned a great salary but were always living pay cheque to pay cheque. There was always a great restaurant to try, a pair of shoes to die for or an event to go to ... you get the gist. Life was great and they were always having a grand time. Until life wasn't great. One day, their car broke down at a set of lights, in peak-hour traffic. Somehow, they managed to get the car to the mechanic and found out a rather costly new engine was required. This cost was placed on their credit card. Not long after, another unexpected hefty dental bill came through. This was also placed on the credit card.

They didn't see it as a big problem as they still earned a good income and paid the repayments on time. But the interest continued to compound. With no savings, and no adjustments to their lifestyle, you can imagine how quickly these unexpected bills added pressure on top of their normal spending. Over time, making the repayments on time became an issue. All of this added stress to their everyday life.

Don't worry, there is a happy ending to the story! Fortunately, my friend did have a light-bulb moment and made the decision to start thinking about money and tackle this mounting debt. It wasn't easy though. But they committed to putting more structure to their spending, and budgeting helped them to start putting money away every month so that when another unexpected life moment happened, it would not be so stressful.

For those of you who have a tendency to squirrel away all of your money and saving isn't something you have to think about, you just naturally do it, it's still just as important to strike a balance between financial security and enjoying the present day. If you don't allow yourself the freedom to treat yourself and actually enjoy the fruits of your hard work, what's the point? After all, the essence of life itself is living. Money is just a tool to help us live a life that is about creating memorable moments. It's all about balance.

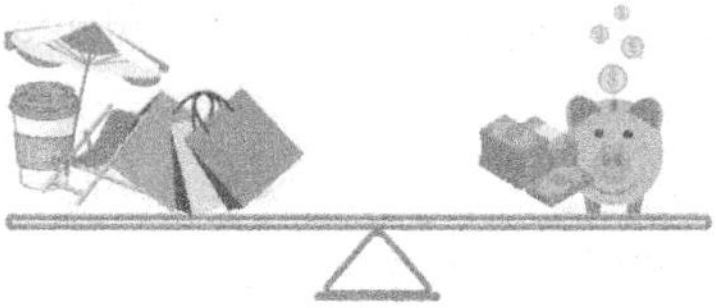

If you're not a natural saver, then start by setting aside a small amount. We talked about 20% in the previous chapter. If this is too much to start with, try a smaller percentage and gradually increase this amount over time. The important thing is to get started and make saving a non-negotiable part of your routine.

8 money saving tips to get you started

- Keep your eye on the prize.

  Let's go back to the goals we talked about earlier in this book. Knowing what you're saving for, how much you need and when you need it by is going to help keep you motivated and give you something to work towards.

- Cut back on your 'want to haves'.

  Do you have a membership to Netflix, Stan, Disney+, Amazon Prime and Foxtel? Do you really need all of them? Could you consider cancelling that gym membership if you never go anyway? Can you use a generic brand rather than a name brand for things? Looking at your budget will help you decide on what the 'want to haves' are.

- Buy second hand.

  Gumtree, eBay and Facebook Marketplace are great places to get some treasures at bargain prices. My greatest online purchase was some $20 dining chairs I bought because I needed something cheap and cheerful. Imagine my surprise when I found out they were actually Italian designer chairs worth $1700!

  These online marketplaces are also great for making money too, by getting rid of the stuff you have laying around that you never use. Isn't that how the Nasty Gal empire got started?

- Negotiate your expenses.

  Make it a habit to regularly review your bill providers, such as your utilities, internet and mobile phone plans. Do a comparison with others online, ask for a discount from your existing provider. This will make sure you're getting the best value for money and give you a chance to make sure the plan you're on is actually suitable for your current needs.

- Plan your meals.

  Dining out can be expensive and having Uber Eats at your fingertips probably doesn't help either. Try to plan your meals in advance and cook at home as much as possible. When you go to the supermarket, use a shopping list so you don't get tempted by all the options. Why not pack your lunch instead of buying? All this helps you to save on food costs and often has the added benefit of eating healthier. If you think eating at home is anti-social, why not invite some friends around? What a cosy way to spend an evening.

- Go for cheaper entertainment.

  Not everything has to cost money! When I used nearly all of my money to buy my first property, I looked for entertainment options that were still fun but were much cheaper or free. I started hiking more with friends rather than eating brunch (good for the wallet and body – winning!); I borrowed books and movies from the library; and there are always plenty of great community events to attend.

- Watch how those little things add up.

  It's amazing how quickly little things can add up. Whether its money saved or spent! $5 here, $10 there. There are approximately 250 working days a year. If you get a coffee every working day, you're spending about $5 a pop, and that adds up to $1250 a year. What else could you have done with that $1250?

- Consider a high interest savings account.

  If you have money sitting in a standard transaction account, then consider moving your money into a high interest savings account. This is a low-risk investment option – not to mention the compound interest – so the interest you earn on your initial deposit is reinvested and future interest is calculated on the new total = more money!

This is by no means an exhaustive list, just some suggestions to get you started. There are so many wallet-friendly tips out there – DIY, buy in bulk, use coupons, the list goes on!

Let's come back to what's essential for you to be successful in creating this rainy-day savings fund. Little things add up, but so does behaviour. It's all about making those small incremental changes over time to create something significant and saving money is all about consistency. Be consistent in your discipline. Be consistent in your habits.

TAKE CHARGE

What are some of your saving goals? What are you working towards, and by when?

What are three things you can change about your lifestyle to better your savings effort? Can you use the money saving tips? Have a brainstorm!

Don't forget to look through your budget and identify areas where you can make some improvements.

Fourth thing – avoid the 'pay later' temptation

When a good friend of mine first entered a relationship with his now wife, he said the hardest thing was to tell her about his credit card debt. As a seemingly intelligent man, he was embarrassed to admit he had allowed himself to get into so much debt – and how this debt just continued to get bigger. It had been so easy to set up an account and so easy to spend the money. His credit card gave him access to this magical fountain of money that never seemed to stop flowing and the low minimum monthly repayment made it the perfect solution for funding his lifestyle.

There are many other people in the same boat. Credit card revenue in the Australian market was $6.1 billion dollars in 2022 alone.[14] The global market for credit card revenue was just over $138 billion in 2020, and this number is expected to grow to $263 billion by 2028.[15] This is a good money-making machine.

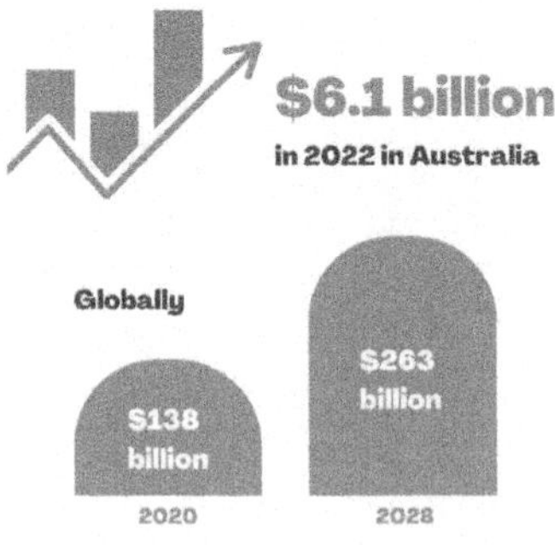

It may seem like an odd thing to say, but I don't think credit cards are all bad. If you are treating your credit card like a debit card and paying the full amount off every month, you can use it to your advantage. If you want to reward yourself with those 100,000 airline points when you open up a new account or get cash back on purchases, it might even be working in your favour.

BUT ... there's a big BUT here. Credit can be good if you use it responsibly. Unfortunately, many of us are not responsible with it.

Credit cards allow you to spend your future money; you get to enjoy the spending now and the future you is responsible for paying it off. This is problematic because we tend to treat our future selves as somewhat different people.[16] This might mean that we prioritise immediate gratification over what's better for us in the long run or underestimate our future needs and not plan ahead properly. It's like choosing to relax on the couch instead of exercising, even though we know exercise is good for us or taking on high-interest debt on a non-essential item. There's also the 'payment coupling' phenomenon, where there is a time difference between the decision to buy something and actually paying for it.[17] This means we don't feel the immediate impact of buying something, so it doesn't feel like we are spending as much money all at once. This is quite a common practise for most online purchases. This dangerous combination makes it a little too easy to spend beyond our means.

A lot of financial institutions and banks put tantalising incentives in place so you can earn points, get free products, earn airline points or even convert it into cash. Believe it or not, they're not doing this out of the goodness of their hearts. Banks and credit card providers spend a fortune in marketing dollars to attract customers every year. You only have look at credit card advertising to see happy faces having fun and the glamorous life you could be having if you were paying with your credit card.

It is easy to fall into the trap of thinking this is quick money. Or sometimes people can't help it and use credit cards to get themselves out of money trouble, especially when it comes to unexpected bills. Unfortunately, that's the worst time and place to use credit cards.

How do credit cards make their money?

First, let's take a look at how they make their profit.

Credit cards are typically issued by financial institutions or banks to customers. Once approved, the issuing entity extends a line of credit to you, the customer. The credit card limit is the maximum the customer can borrow. So how do these entities make their money?

- **Transaction fees** – whenever you make a purchase, the business you're buying from pays a percentage of the purchase to the card network (e.g. Mastercard, Visa) and to the issuing entity. You may have noticed the pesky 1–2% fees that retailers and hospitality venues charge when you're paying by card.
- **Interest charges** – if you don't pay off the balance by the due date, interest charges are applied to the remaining balance. This is usually the biggest stream of revenue for these financial entities. Many credit cardholders get into trouble as the interest rates are typically very high. Since the interest rate is applied to the remaining balance, the amount owing can grow quickly if you don't pay on time.
- **Annual fees** – some credit cards charge an annual fee. The amount depends on the type of card and the benefits. Usually the bigger the reward, the higher the fee.
- **Penalty fees** – let's not forget about the various penalty fees – i.e. if you exceed your credit limit, didn't make the payment on time or used the card for cash advances.

As you can see, there are plenty of ways for financial entities and card networks to make money from their customers.

So if you are a credit card holder, be aware of the high interest rates, late fees and whether you are likely to be responsible with using a credit card. Be honest with yourself, can you trust yourself to not over-indulge? Are the rewards worth the yearly fees you're paying? Do you really need the credit card? If the answer is no to any of these questions, then you might be doing yourself a favour by not getting one and removing the enticement altogether.

Nowadays, some debit cards have many of the same benefits and facilities as credit cards, not to mention lower transaction fees. So that might be a better option if you feel you might be tempted to overspend on a credit card.

If you need another incentive for not getting a credit card – if you are wanting to get into the property market, mortgage lenders take your credit card into consideration. They will look at your credit card limit and multiply this limit with a factor. Lenders assess this as a liability as it could reduce your ability to make repayments. The higher your limit is, the lower your borrowing limit can be.

Buy now, pay later (BNPL)

BNPL is the latest type of payment scheme that has been introduced over the years. It is a type of short-term financing. This is sort of like using a credit card but without doing an application or using a card. Some of the providers don't even do a credit check! It seems a little too convenient – no credit application, four small payments AND no interest?

How do they even make money? Well, not our problem. As long as they are giving us these sweet deals, right? Well. Sort of.

Most of the income they make comes from the fees they charge the retailers that use them. But these retailers are smart. They know their customers and know them well. They know their customers might not make a purchase if there is no BNPL option available. These retailers have a profit to make!

Even though the BNPL services are marketed as no interest, they do charge fees for late repayments. The appeal of small repayments, combined with getting your hands on the purchased items immediately – you can see how it could easily lead to losing control of your spending. Some stats for you to ponder:

- According to the Financial Wellbeing study conducted by ANZ in 2023,

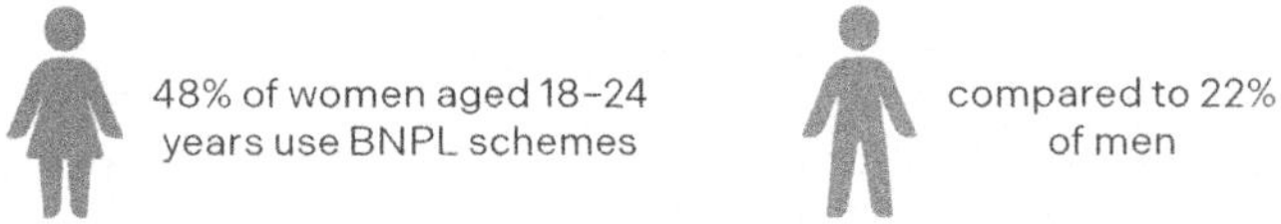

- Afterpay is considered to be the biggest BNPL service provider. If we used their data as a benchmark

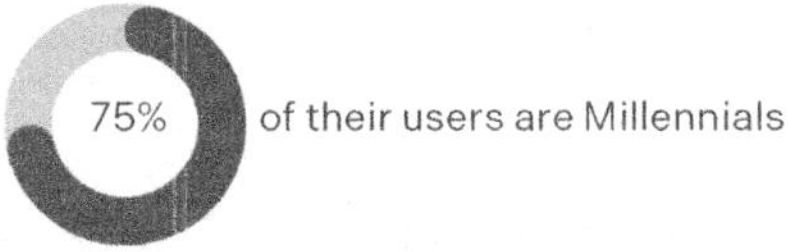

- In the latest ASIC study, they have found that

As little as those repayments seem at time of purchase, it can easily lead to overspending and accumulating bad debt.

A friend of mine shared a story with me about her sister getting sucked into these BNPL companies. Her dad gave her a credit card to use while she was at university and stressed it was only to be used for emergencies and essentials. She was pretty good with it for a while. In fact, she only ever used it a couple of times for some untimely bills. That was until she discovered BNPL. Like many others during the pandemic, she had extra time on her hands and spent a lot of time looking at things online. She found that once unaffordable items seemed very affordable when split into four small instalments. She ended up buying all sorts of things and didn't notice how quickly the payments all piled up. The credit card was maxed out in just over two months. She had to swallow her pride and make that dreaded call to her parents. They gave her a stern talking to but decided to help her pay off the credit card debt and set up a plan for her to pay them back.

Her sister got lucky. She had the financial backing of her parents. Many people do not have this luxury. It is easy to overspend if you are only looking at those small individual instalments. You are really paying for instant gratification big time. I hate to think how many people got into debt during the pandemic, when people increased their online shopping habit to curb the boredom.

Once again, for those of you that are wanting to get into the property market, mortgage lenders don't love BNPL transactions on your record either. I remember I was finalising the paperwork for a mortgage and thought everything was on track for final sign off, until my bank broker called me in a panic to ask me to provide evidence of my Afterpay repayments. I had used Afterpay to pay for a $20 item many months prior, because they were having a promotion where they provided a $10 discount for any purchase. I can tell you now, that $10 was definitely not worth all the hassle I had to go through with the bank.

TAKE CHARGE

Are you using credit cards or BNPL services? If so, make sure you're reviewing your statements on a regular basis.

Make sure you understand the terms of the application. Yes, that means reading as much of the fine print as you can. Do you know exactly what interest is being charged? What about the fees? Are you using a credit card because of the reward program? Have you calculated if the benefit you get outweighs the amount of money you are paying for using the credit card, e.g. annual fees?

Have you searched for a normal transaction account with similar benefits as your credit card?

Fifth thing – have an insurance umbrella ready on a rainy day

I used to think of insurance as an evil, unnecessary expense. Why should I pay monthly premiums for something I never use or claim? Why couldn't I use that for groceries instead?

But someone very wise said to me how I should consider myself lucky if I never have to make an insurance claim. It's a safety net you are lucky to have for those 'just in case' moments. I must admit that is a different way of thinking – and true as well.

Insurance is like having an umbrella on a stormy day. It might feel a little annoying to carry one around when it's not raining. But once a downpour starts, it's going to shield and protect you from the worst of it.

I don't know about you, but I always felt a lot more carefree when it was just me. But once you have a partner or a family, it's no longer just you that you have to worry about, it's your entire family unit. None of us have a crystal ball to tell the future; sometimes bad things happen to good people. If insurance can at least step in to help and remove some of the stress, when the sh*t does hit the fan, it's almost a no-brainer.

There are many types of insurances to make your life easier – health insurance, life insurance, income protection insurance ... the list goes on. Before you sign up for every single insurance to protect all aspects of your life and your neighbour's, why not start with a little homework first – which ones do you actually need? You want to make sure you have the right cover for you. You want to have protection, but the right amount of protection as there's no point in going overboard. I'm sure you don't want to be driving with a safety belt *and* wearing a helmet *and* shin pads *and* a mouthguard. Well ... I mean, you might, but it seems to be a little excessive for a drive to the shops.

So, which insurances might be worth exploring for you?

Life, TPD, income protection insurances through superannuation

If you're an employee, chances are you're eligible for superannuation through your employer. Many of us have life insurance and total and permanent disability (TPD) insurance automatically through our superannuation, and some of us also have income protection insurance in our superannuation.

- **Life,** also known as **death cover** insurance – provides a lump sum/income to your beneficiary or beneficiaries if you die or have a terminal illness.
- **Total and permanent disability** insurance – provides a payout to you if you become totally and permanently disabled because of injury or illness.

- **Income protection** insurance – provides you with a monthly payment to cover part of your income for a specific time period if you become ill or injured and can't work. It doesn't provide any cover if you resign or unexpectedly lose your job.

Most of us will have these insurances through our superannuation, but some of us choose to have these as standalone insurances outside our superannuation. There are some pros and cons of doing it this way.

Pros of insurance through your superannuation	Cons of insurance through your superannuation
• Automated payments from your superannuation. Since these are taken straight from your super balance, you don't need to make any extra repayments. • Premiums are usually cheaper. Since most super funds buy these in bulk, this means you benefit from cheaper premiums. • Less health checks required. Most of the policies through super will provide you with a default cover without any health checks. • More tax effective. The premium is paid from your pre-tax income. These are only taxed at 15% within the fund, as compared to your **marginal tax rate** (typically much higher than this).	• You don't have a say in the type of cover you get. The policies are not personalised for you and the cover is likely to be basic. • Reduces retirement savings. The premiums will reduce your super balance. • The proceeds may be taxed depending on the circumstances, compared with if you have these insurances outside super, then the proceeds are usually not taxed. • Insurance may be cancelled. If your super account becomes inactive, if you changed supers or stopped contributing, then your cover could end – leaving you without any insurance protection.

MARGINAL TAX RATE

Your marginal tax rate is the percentage of tax you pay on each additional dollar of income.

Health insurance

Australia has a great public healthcare system in place. In 2021, it ranked third overall in the Commonwealth Fund healthcare report and first for equity and healthcare outcomes.[18] Medicare provides access to essential services and treatments for many of us, including public hospital care, GP visits and subsidised medications. With this in mind, why do you still need private health insurance?

Private health insurance offers additional choices and benefits beyond what Medicare can offer. Not to mention the Medicare levy surcharge and Lifetime Health Cover loading. At the time of writing, you have to pay for a surcharge based on the following:

- If you are a single person earning more than $93,000 taxable income per year.
- If you are a family or couple earning more than $186,000 taxable income per year; this threshold increases by $1,500 for each child after the first.
- If you do not have appropriate hospital cover with your health insurance.

Single income	$93,000 or less	$ 93,001 – $108,000	$108,001 – $144,000	$144,001 or more
Couples/ family income	$186,000 or less	$186,001 – $216,000	$216,001 – $288,000	$288,001 or more
Medicare levy surcharge	0%	1%	1.25%	1.5%

Once you reach the age of 31, Lifetime Health Cover loading kicks in. This is a government initiative to encourage people to sign up to private health insurance earlier in life, rather than waiting until they are older. So basically for every year you don't have hospital cover, an extra 2% is added to your insurance premium. To avoid this cost, you can get hospital cover before 1st July following your 31st birthday.

There are plenty of options to consider when you're taking out a policy – Hospital cover only, Hospitals and Extras, different co-pay amounts, various coverage benefits, all leading to different premiums paid. To do a comparison with different policies and providers, check out www.privatehealth.gov.au.

Home and contents insurance

It is estimated that 60% of Australians have Home and Contents insurance to protect their homes. Of this 60%, about 80% underinsure their homes. So not enough of us are insuring our homes, and even if we do, we're not insuring it for the correct amount.

Home and Contents insurance can help pay for damages to your house or belongings in the case of insured events such as theft, fire or storm. The sum of the insured amount is the amount you would like your home to be covered for. This isn't just the value of your house; it is the total amount to rebuild your house to its current state if it is destroyed. Building costs increase over time so you will need to revisit this figure every so often.

Shop around a little for the best deal, especially when your policy is coming to an end. Make a habit of reading through the product disclosure statements for your policies as well, so you know exactly what your policy covers. Sure, they might be long and boring to go through, but they provide you with important information that allows you to do a fair comparison between providers and know exactly what entitlements are offered.

On the topic of getting the best deal, nobody likes to pay for high premiums every year. Rather than knowingly underinsuring, there are other tactics you can use to get the best bang for buck. What about considerations such as increasing your excess, installing indoor and outdoor alarms, combining your policies for a discount and getting your insurance online?

If you own investment properties, don't forget landlord insurance. This is essential to protect your property and potential loss of income from the property.

Car insurance

There are over 20 million cars registered in Australia; that means there's a lot of cars on the road! You may be the best driver around, but you can't control the actions of others sharing the road with you. Not everyone has the same level of expertise or caution.

There are four main types of car insurances you may want to explore further: comprehensive, third-party property damage, third-party fire and theft, and compulsory third party.

Whether you drive the latest Tesla or an old clunker from the 1980s, you need car insurance to make sure you're covered in the case of an accident. But be sure to crunch the numbers to ensure you have the right cover.

Type of insurance	Comprehensive	Third-party, fire & theft	Third-party property	Compulsory third party
Injuries or death	No	No	No	✓
Damage to other people's property	✓	✓	✓	No
Damage or loss of your car caused by theft or fire	✓	✓	No	No
Damage to your car from a traffic accident	✓	No	No	No

Source: https://www.canstar.com.au/car-insurance/types-of-car-insurance/

Pet insurance

With just under 70% of households having a pet, Australia has one of the highest rates of pet ownership in the world. Dogs are the most common, followed by cats. These furry companions never judge your dance moves, give you free therapy sessions and fill your heart with more love than sense. It is our duty to shower them with affection, treats and ensure their wellbeing in return. While many pet owners are aware of the expense of owning a pet, pet insurance isn't very common with only 7% of pets covered.

It is a way to remove some of the financial burden if your pet does get hurt or sick, as it can get rather expensive. A friend of mine spent $5000 for minor surgery for her dog. Pet insurance definitely worked out for her because the insurance covered the majority of the cost. Plus, you wouldn't believe how many allergies this dog had!

Do your homework around the insurance type, coverage benefits and monthly premiums and know what the exclusions are. Perhaps a better consideration might be putting the same amount of money that you would pay for pet insurance into a high interest savings account and withdraw funds as you need for your furry companion.

How much insurance do I need?

There are many other types of insurance that we haven't covered here – such as travel insurance, professional indemnity insurance and business insurance, etc. Jump online and start reading.

Remember having insurance is about peace of mind, but it's also about balance. It's about wearing a safety belt to make sure you are protected, but one that is not going to strain your finances unnecessarily, so that your rainy-day fund remains intact.

TAKE CHARGE

Take time to assess your needs and think about what you value most and use this to work out what insurances you need. Whether it's ensuring your earnings are safeguarded with income protection insurance, looking after your belongings with contents insurance, or having the right level of health insurance.

Make sure you shop around to find the best policy possible. There are always multiple providers as well as multiple policies to choose from.

If you already have insurance for a few things, then when was the last time you did a review? Are you still on the right cover for your current situation? Are the limits appropriate?

Have you got a reminder to notify you when your policies are due? Why not create a calendar reminder to prompt you to shop around for the best value and make sure the information on your policy is up to date?

Sixth thing – leave your mark with estate planning

Estate planning is how you get to decide what happens to you and your stuff when you're no longer around on planet Earth – or no longer have the capacity to make decisions for yourself.

You can provide exact instructions on how your assets are to be passed on to your loved ones and how you would like things to be taken care of. While I'm not trying to give you an existential crisis with thoughts of your imminent demise, it wouldn't hurt to have a master plan ready for life's grand finale. You may think – I have plenty of time, I'm fit and healthy, there's no point in thinking about this now.

According to estate planning experts, if you say 'yes' to any of the following then it is not too early to plan for your legacy:

- Over the age of 18
- Have a spouse/partner
- Own assets
- Have dependents.

Will and testamentary trust

Most people think estate planning is having a will. Estate planning is a lot more than that, but having a will is an essential part. Just as you put sunscreen on before the start of a day to prevent sunburn (sunscreen is recommended for daily use by the way – apparently, it's the number one anti-ageing product!), planning ahead is a priority.

> It is estimated that over half of Australians die without having a will in place.

If you don't have a will in place, or a valid will in place, this is called 'dying intestate'.

When this happens, the process becomes more complex. Here are some of the downsides of not having a will:

- Higher legal fees as dealing with an estate without a will can be more time consuming and complex.
- You will have no control over how your assets will be distributed.
- There can be delays in asset distribution to your family and loved ones.
- You are likely to pay more in taxes as there may be little tax planning and asset distribution in place.

You can imagine how much more stress it's going to add to your loved ones during an already difficult time. Your will is like your sunscreen – not only does it protect your legacy; it also protects any potential 'burns' that might come up after you're gone.

Getting a will done is relatively straightforward. It would be worthwhile to consult a solicitor or a public trustee. There are even online will kits available nowadays. However, if you are unsure or your situation is a little complex, e.g. if you are in a blended family with kids from previous relationships or marriages, it is definitely worth your time to consult a professional.

Important: Your will can only contain assets you personally own, or things held as tenants in common.

TENANTS IN COMMON

Type of co-ownership where two or more people can own a property together, but can have equal or different shares of that property.

What might you consider including in your will?

- How you would like to distribute your assets among your beneficiaries, like your family, friends and charities
- Who will look after your children or pets
- Plans for your funeral
- Plans for your digital legacy like your social media accounts
- Executor/s of estate to carry out the instructions of your will
- Any trusts you want to set up.

Taxes, money and your estate

While there is no inheritance tax in Australia, there are other taxes to be aware of. So if your beneficiary inherits assets, there are no taxes to pay. But if your beneficiaries sell these inherited assets, there may be capital gains tax (CGT) to pay, although this is not always the case depending on the asset. For example, if you are planning to pass on your primary residence as an inheritance and your beneficiaries decide to sell it within two years of inheriting it, then no CGT applies.

> **CAPTIAL GAINS TAX**
> Profit made from selling assets.

Another area to be aware of is the taxation of your superannuation benefits. If your superannuation pays benefits to those who are not financially dependent on you, your beneficiaries may be subject to taxes when they inherit these benefits. For example, adult children may face a 17% tax on the concessional component of the superannuation benefits and a higher 32% tax on any life insurance component.

Before any assets can be distributed to your beneficiaries, debts must be paid down first by using the funds available in your estate. There is secured debt (e.g. mortgage) and unsecured debt (e.g. credit cards). If there is not enough money to pay the debt, the executor may need to sell assets to pay it down before your beneficiaries can receive anything.

Testamentary trust

A testamentary trust is a trust created within a will, after death, that helps to manage and distribute assets in a smart and tax-efficient way for your beneficiaries. It's similar to a family discretionary trust, but part

> **FAMILY DISCRETIONARY TRUST**
> A way to hold family assets for the beneficiaries, with the trustee/s having the discretion to decide how to distribute assets to them.

of a will, so it only comes into effect when someone has passed away. (Family discretionary trust is established and activated when someone is still alive).

It can be a great way to pass on wealth in a controlled manner. Rather than giving assets directly to your beneficiaries, the assets are placed in a trust and your beneficiaries are in charge of the trust. This can be useful when beneficiaries are young, have disabilities or are in need of careful management of their inheritance. There is also the option to include a clause to make sure that only your direct descendants can benefit, e.g. your children or grandchildren. It can also offer protection of the assets against legal action for your beneficiaries, such as money troubles or divorce.

If your beneficiary is under 18 years old, a testamentary trust can provide tax advantages by allowing the income from the trust to be distributed to them at adult tax rates. The income of someone under 18 years of age is sometimes taxed at a higher rate than an adult. There's also the benefit of the standard tax-free threshold of $18,200 (at time of writing).

Of course, very few things in this world are free. Trust set up and maintenance cost money. Trusts are complex and you are likely to have to pay fees for accounting and other fees, so that's something to note.

Your executors have a crucial role to play, so it may be wise to talk to the person (or persons) that you are choosing as your executor and let them know what you want, so they can make sure your wishes are carried out exactly the way you want.

Your life changes over time, so this should also be reflected in your will. A good habit may be to review it at least every few years. Your will should be updated when big things happen in your life, particularly changes that impact your money situation, such as getting married, divorced or having kids. For example, when you get married, your old will becomes invalid unless you specifically mention getting married ('Contemplation of Marriage' clause – if you marry after making the will, your new spouse is entitled to inherit, even if they weren't named in the will originally) in it.

Power of attorney

Power of attorney is a document that gives someone else the right to act on your behalf in legal and financial matters. This includes making decisions and managing your affairs related to your estate in case you become incapacitated or are unable to handle your own affairs.

General power of attorney: this provides the appointed person the authority to manage your financial and legal affairs for a specific period of time, or until you revoke it. This is common when you need someone to handle things for you temporarily, e.g. if you're travelling overseas. A general power of attorney is no longer valid if you can't make decisions for yourself.

Enduring power of attorney: this remains valid even if you no longer have the mental capacity or become incapacitated. This is common for estate planning to make sure someone can manage your affairs when you can't do it yourself. It is vital to establish this while you have the mental capacity to make decisions and fully understand the implications.

Enduring power of guardianship

This document allows another person to make decisions on your lifestyle, medical treatment and care on your behalf when you are no longer able to. The person you appoint as your enduring guardian is obligated to make decisions they believe align with your choices.

Advanced Care Directive

'Advanced Care Directive' or 'Living Will' – you are likely to hear a few variations on the name, depending on which state you live in. This document is different to that of the enduring power of guardianship. This allows you to provide exact instructions around the medical treatment you want, especially if you have strong preferences for your future healthcare.

* * * *

With all of these documents/appointments, it is important to speak to the person/s you are entrusting to make decisions on your behalf so they can follow your exact wishes. Don't forget to seek information and advice from a professional. They will help to provide guidance on your specific individual needs to increase the likelihood of you getting the best possible outcome.

Superannuation

We will cover superannuation in more detail later but including it in your thinking around estate planning can be valuable. Superannuation isn't necessarily part of your estate so it's important for you to tell your superannuation fund who your beneficiaries are. Without clear instructions, the fund trustee will use their own discretion to distribute your death benefit. It is good idea to review and confirm you have beneficiaries listed, and note there are usually three types – binding, non-binding and reversionary. More on this later.

TAKE CHARGE

If you haven't started estate planning yet, now might be a good time to do some preparation. Here are some considerations to get yourself ready for your conversation with a professional.

1. Your estate

   A good place to start is to know what assets you have: properties, business assets, superannuation, shares, life insurance benefits, savings, etc. You may be pleasantly surprised by how much you do have when you start listing everything you own. Compile a list of everything you own in your name and assign value.

Do you have a clear understanding of your finances? This also needs to include your debt, because this needs to be paid off by the money and assets you leave behind in your estate.

Continue with the questions earlier in this section under 'What might you consider including in your will?'

2. Your life and healthcare decisions

   Think about and write down your healthcare preferences and values; consider medical treatment options in different scenarios such as if you become severely ill or are facing an end-of-life situation.

3. Your beneficiaries

   Think about who will receive which assets within your estate.

TAKE CHARGE

If you are in a relationship, it might be natural to leave things to your partner – your assets; the care of your dependants; making decisions on your behalf when you can't. But you also need to consider a backup plan, in the unlikely chance that both of you pass away at the same time.

Your trusted representative

4. Whoever you choose to be the executor of your will, the agent of the power of attorney or your enduring guardian, be aware this is a lot of responsibility for someone. Make sure they are informed of your expectations and are willing and capable of fulfilling those duties.

Seventh thing – pay the right amount of tax: the Goldilocks principle

As the cliché goes, there are only two things certain in life – death and taxes. I can't say I know many people who like taxes – maybe accountants! But you know what, paying tax isn't a bad thing. After all, taxes are an important source of income for the government, and a big contribution to providing essential services and maintaining a functional society. Besides, if you're paying taxes, it shows you're earning an income. I would rather earn an income and pay taxes than have no money and no taxes!

Remember Goldilocks and the three bears? Goldilocks ate the porridge that was neither too hot nor too cold and fell asleep on the bed that was not too hard nor too soft. We want to stick to the same principle with paying taxes. Not too much because there are plenty of other things you would rather do with your money, nor too little because that's tax evasion. You want to pay just the right amount of tax you are legally bound to pay.

The concept of filing tax returns used to rather baffle me. If the government already knew how much tax I should be paying and I could potentially be punished for not paying the correct amount, then why didn't they just do it for me, and we could avoid the whole paperwork business?

Alas, it's not so simple.

If you're a standard wage earner, with your main income source from your primary job, perhaps it's best if you just save your pennies and file your own taxes online. I used to do this myself and it's pretty straightforward. But if you have other sources of income, or there's something quirky about your situation, find a good accountant that specialises in your type of situation. It will be well worth your while. They do this for a living after all! However, no matter how good your accountant is, it's always good to have a basic understanding of what you're entitled to, as the ultimate responsibility is still with you (not your accountant).

How to pay the right amount of tax?

These are some ideas to get you started figuring out how to pay the right amount of tax.

You need to know where you stand. If you are considered an Australian resident for tax purposes, your marginal tax rates are below. As you can see, the tax rates for 2023-24 look quite different from 2024-25. The government introduced these tax rate changes to help with the cost of living.

Rates for 2023–24 financial year		Rates from 2024–25 onwards	
Income	**Tax paid**	**Income**	**Tax paid**
0 – $18,200	Nil	0 – $18,200	Nil
$18,201 – $45,000	19c for each $1 over $18,200	$18,201 – $45,000	16%
$45,001 – $120,000	$5,092 plus 32.5c for each $1 over $45,000	$45,001 – $135,000	30%
$120,001 – $180,000	$29,467 plus 37c for each $1 over $120,000	$135,001 – $190,000	37%
$180,001 and over	$51,667 plus 45c for each $1 over $180,000	$190,001 and over	45%

Figure 2: source – *ATO, 2024 (excludes Medicare levy)*

Having this knowledge will help you with planning. The tax rate is fixed for the income tiers (pending ATO changes), so you can't control that. But you can control how your income fits into these different tiers. You can maximise your deductions and tax benefits, minimise your liability and optimise your strategies. Let's take a closer look ...

Maximise your deductions

This is right in your accountant's wheelhouse. They will help you to maximise any work- or investment-related deductions. You still need to have a basic understanding of what you can claim as a deduction and keep documentation for it so you know what to provide to your accountant. ATO's website is pretty good at explaining the different requirements and providing examples. Things that can be deducted include charitable donations, work-related expenses, washing your uniform, home office expenses etc. Deductions can come with specific nuances, so it's worth going through them to make sure you are making the most of every opportunity. Let's use an example of work-from-home expenses.

Rachel and Monica both have an office set up at home to work and wanted to work out their deductions for the year.

Fixed rate Method

Rachel wanted to use the fixed rate method as it's simpler.

38 hours per week
x
40 working weeks
x
$0.67 per hour
=
$1,018 claimed

Actual cost Method

Monica wanted to use the actual cost method as she was already keeping a diary of her exact hours and keeps a meticulous record of all her bills. The total expenses she paid for the year was $10,000, which includes electricity, gas, etc. The office she works out from is 20% of the home floor space.etc. The office she works out from is 20% of the home floor space.

$10,000
x
20% (office space)
=
$2,000 claimed

This means that Rachel can deduct $1,018 from her taxable income while Monica can deduct $2,000 in that tax year. The actual tax benefit for both depends on their marginal tax rate – if Monica's tax rate is 37%, then the tax benefit would be $740 (37% of $2000).

While this example is simplified and fictious, it gives you an indication of the potential tax benefits you are entitled to if you put in a bit of effort and explore further. You also need to weigh up the reward vs. effort – if it is going to take you two hours every week to keep tabs of expenses, is it worth the benefit?

If you have investments, there are deductions for the costs associated with managing them, e.g. the interest portion of your investment property's mortgage or the financial advisory fees for buying stocks in the share market.

If you are a freelancer or business owner, there are even more expenses you are able to deduct from your taxable income – business-related travel costs, professional fees, office supplies, etc. There may also be specific concessions just for you, like immediate reductions for specific asset purchases and simplified depreciation rules.

Keeping detailed records is crucial for claiming deductions. It will help you be prepared for any potential questions or audits from the ATO.

Maximise your tax benefits

There are even more things you can do to optimise your tax position. Have you considered these savvy strategies?

- Make extra superannuation contributions. Pre-tax (concessional) contributions are generally taxed at a lower rate, i.e. at 15%, compared to your marginal tax rate. After-tax (non-concessional) contributions can also be a good way to grow your money in a super account. When you're making non-concessional contributions, you're putting after-tax money into your super account, so this money has already been taxed. This means that any earnings generated in the super account are usually tax-free. One thing to be aware of is the 'contribution cap', which is a limit to how much you can contribute every year without having to pay extra taxes. Make sure you go through the chapter about superannuation later in the book to find out more about concessional and non-concessional limits. Use the contributions in a clever way to work to your advantage, so you don't miss out! Let's look at an example:

Cara wants to supercharge her superannuation account this year. Her annual income is $100,000 a year, and she makes a total concessional contribution of $25,000 towards her superannuation account in this financial year.

Superannuation

Cara's superannuation got a net boost of $21,250

(15% concessional tax = $3,750)
$25,000 – $3,750 = $21,250)

She can also claim a tax deduction for the $25,000, which brings her taxable income to $75,000 so now she gets to pay $8,125 less in tax

($100,000 income x 32.5% tax rate
– $75,000 new income x 32.5%)

Cara's net tax saving is $4,375 ($8,125 – $3,750)
A tax savings and a superannuation boost = win win!

- Take advantage of the franking credit system. If one of your investment strategies is to receive dividends from your stocks, then companies that pay franked dividends have already paid tax on that money. The ATO recognises this and you won't be taxed twice.

- For example: Benjamin is a full-time stay-at-home dad and his partner Natasha is the main provider. They bought shares in companies that give their investors franked dividends and credits, all under Benjamin's name. During the year, Benjamin received $5,000 in fully franked dividends, plus $5,000 in franking credits. This means not only does he receive $5,000 in dividends, but he will also receive $5,000 in tax refund for the credits, as his marginal tax rate is at 0%.

- Holding investments in tax-effective structures, such as in a family trust or in your superannuation can also help to manage income generated and capital gains tax. For example: Natasha and Benjamin have a trust that holds assets that produce $50,000 in income every year. The income can be split among the members within a family trust. Since Natasha is the main income provider earning $200,000 a year, they may choose to allocate the $50,000 to Benjamin to minimise the total tax on the investment income.

- And let's just say that you're holding an investment in your superannuation, any capital gains made from that investment is not only usually taxed at a lower rate, but may even be tax-free when your superannuation is at the retirement phase.

Did you know that the Australian Government provides a scheme called LITO? LITO stands for Low-Income Tax Offset. These offsets help to reduce the tax you have to pay. The bonus is that you don't have to do anything to take advantage of the offset, it's automatic.

Income	Maximum offset
0 - $37,500	$700
$37,501 and $45,000	$700 minus 5 cents for every $1 above $37,500
$45,001 and $66,667	$325 minus 1.5 cents for every $1 above $45,000

Figure 3: *source - ATO, 2023*

Time your gains and losses

Timing can also make a significant difference in reducing your tax liability. Carefully balancing your expenses and income, capital gains and losses can help to leverage things in your favour. Business owners tend to have more flexibility, as if you are an employee, your income is more or less set by your employer. But if you can, then it is definitely pursuing! Let's use a simple example to look at how timing can make a difference.

Morgan is a high-earner who's earning $200,000 in the current financial year. Due to a change in her circumstances, her gross income will be $80,000 for the next financial year. If Morgan can defer some of the income ($30,000) from the current year to the next financial year, she can have a tax 'savings' of $2,950!

Current situation

	Current year	Next year
Income	$ 200,000	$ 80,000
Tax	$ 60,667	$ 16,467
Total tax for both years		$ 77,134

By deferring $30,000 of income to the next financial year

Current year (new income)	Next year (new income)	
$ 170,000	$ 110,000	
$ 47,967	$ 26,217	
		$ 2,950
	$ 74,184	less tax paid

This is the same with timing for capital gains. You are likely to pay CGT on any profit when you sell or dispose of an asset. Let's say you have certain investments to sell but are not sure when to do it. One thing you are sure of is the profit is going to be sky high. It may be a good idea to pick a time when your income is on the lower side so capital gains is a bit more friendly on your wallet. This is the same for a capital loss – you may wish to balance this out with a big income year.

Let's use Morgan's numbers again. Let's say she is selling an asset that will have a profit of $25,000.

	Earning $200,000 per year		Earning $80,000 per year	
	Didn't sell asset	**Sold asset**	**Didn't sell asset**	**Sold asset**
Profit from asset	$ 0	$ 25,000	$ 0	$ 25,000
Total income	$ 200,000	$ 225,000	$ 80,000	$ 105,000
Tax paid	$ 60,667	$ 71,917	$ 16,467	$ 24,592

Look at the difference this makes! Forward planning can potentially save you thousands of dollars!

Also – don't forget about the CGT discount. By holding an investment asset for over 12 months, you may be eligible for a discount of 50%.

I recommend talking to a good accountant to help you do things right and get things in order when it comes to investments. This could potentially save you a lot of money and headaches. Make sure you have discussions early and not after the fact, as by then it's usually too late to make a difference.

TAKE CHARGE

Are you familiar with what deductions you are entitled to?

Review your taxable income and work with your accountant to check areas you can optimise and learn more about.

How are you maximising your deductions or benefits?

work hard for you. By investing wisely, you can be in charge of how you live your life. When you're in control financially, you're the one calling the shots. This is why I am passionate about investing.

Why too much cash in the bank isn't good for you

Unless you're Scrooge McDuck, you don't need to swim in your riches every day, so having too much money in the bank is not a good thing. Why don't we want too much cash around? The shortest answer to this is – inflation.

Inflation is the increase in prices over time. Australia's central bank, the Reserve Bank of Australia, aims for an inflation target between 2–3% each year to keep overall price levels in the economy stable. If it falls below this range, it can lead to a price decrease over time. You may think 'yay, cheaper stuff', but it can be harmful to the economy as it can discourage investment and spending. But if inflation is higher than the target, it can lead to higher living costs and reduced purchasing power.

If your money is just sitting there in the bank, inflation will eat away at the value of your money, making it worth less as prices increase over time. Five dollars 20 years ago can buy a lot more than five dollars today!

To protect your money from losing value, it is essential to find investments that can make more money than inflation takes away.

I wish I had understood the power of investment earlier. When I was growing up, finances were not usually a topic of discussion at the dinner table. My parents always emphasised the importance of studying hard to get a secure, well-paying job. They believed in living within your means and have enough leftover each month. Then you're set for life, in their books.

My dad did dabble in the stock market once. He invested money in two companies based on recommendations from his friends. Unfortunately, things didn't go as planned. One company went into liquidation, and the other one lost 50% of its value within a few short months. My mum then banned share investing in our house and we didn't talk about it again. (Lesson alert – do your research and don't go by hearsay.)

That was the extent of my investing knowledge for most of my teens. In my mind, investing was for rich people who had money to spare. My idea of a secure financial future was to put away money every single month so I had enough for retirement. I believed this for the longest time, even once I started investing.

Towards the end of my time at high school, I became friends with a guy who would sporadically talk about the share market and how his shares were doing. I couldn't believe it. He was only 17 years old! How did he know anything about investing in shares? He explained his parents believed in the importance of teaching him basic financial skills from a young age. They encouraged him to save his pocket money and the money he earned from his after-school job and put them to good use. He used that money to invest in shares. It wasn't a huge amount of money, but it was something. I just remember being amazed that someone my age, someone no smarter than me, had this knowledge and was investing. Maybe it wasn't just for wealthy people after all.

I wish I could say this experience transformed me and propelled me to invest my every spare dollar, setting me up as a hotshot investor. But it didn't. I didn't get pocket money and my after-school job gave me a rather measly amount each week. But it definitely sparked an interest and made me think about investing once I had a more regular income stream.

There are many different ways to invest your money and possibilities to explore when it comes to wealth building. You might think about purchasing assets like shares, real estate or commodities. You could consider entering into ventures, such as business. The outcome should be the same – potential passive income and growth on your investment over time, while you are busy living your day-to-day life.

Be mindful, though. There are many get-rich-quick schemes out there, and usually the only people who are getting rich are the people that are spruiking it. Make sure you do your homework before putting any money down. While investing does have risks, it also has equal opportunity for reward. The level of risk and return associated depends on factors such as asset class, market conditions and your risk tolerance.

Beyond making smart decisions, we should also be mindful of the nuances between the way females and males approach and handle finances and investments. A 2018 HSBC study[19] showed that while women tend to take care of the day-to-day finances, men took a lead in investing. According to a more recent 2023 study:

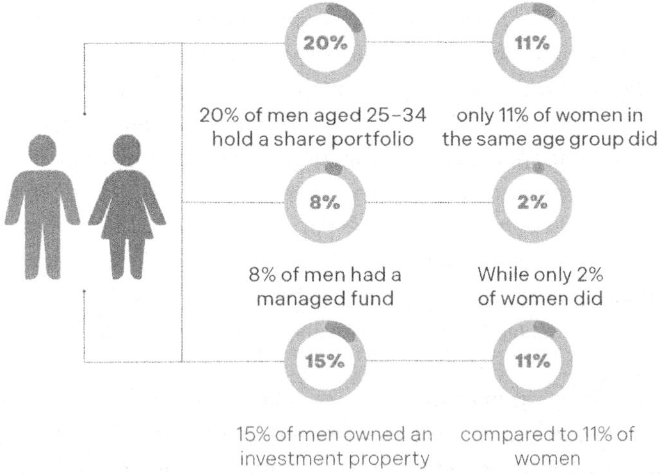

These numbers show that more men seem to be in the investment game than women. Financial knowledge and lack of financial confidence were the number one reasons why women invested less. This knowledge gap is likely to lead some of us to be more hesitant or reluctant to explore investment opportunities, perhaps thinking that investing is complex and risky. Throughout the rest of the chapter, we will cover some key investment concepts, introduce different assets and decode some jargon.

One critical fact before we move on - you don't need to know everything from the start. Analysis paralysis is real and you don't want to fall into the trap. A better approach may be to focus on building a foundation of knowledge and learning as you go. You don't need to be sprinting at full speed at day zero. You have to learn to walk before you can run, and you have to crawl before you can walk.

Start with the basics, put your learnings into action and expand your knowledge along the way. The more you know, the better actions you will take and the more confident you will be as an investor.

Diversity is key

To make your money work for you, it doesn't have to be singing, dancing and flashing. We have all heard about the multi-million- or billion-dollar investments. But the truth is, it just doesn't happen that often. Because most of the people in the world are not that rich.

Make diversification a key consideration in your investment plan because it helps to spread out risks and maximise potential returns.

By investing across different asset classes, sectors and geographic areas, you can help to reduce the impact of any single investment. The saying 'Don't put all of your eggs in one basket' is a good investment strategy to a T. Diversification is like having multiple delectables on your plate to feast on; even if one thing tastes bad, there are still plenty of other options to tickle your taste buds.

Not only is diversification good for protecting you from potential losses, it can also introduce you to potentially unfamiliar investment options. It's like when you're trying new foods and discovering flavours you never knew existed. By investing in new areas, you can learn about opportunities in different assets. This will increase your knowledge and experience, and who knows, you might discover an investment opportunity that becomes a favourite and contributes significantly to your overall financial success.

This is certainly true for me. Dabbling with small amounts in different areas has allowed me to find investment options I'm passionate about.

Risk profile

Investment and risk go hand in hand. Even though they don't have to be fantastical, all investments do carry some element of risk.

Each of us has our own risk profile. Some of us are comfortable taking a higher risk for higher potential returns and some of us like a more cautious approach. Understanding your own risk profile is crucial in helping you to make decisions that align with your own circumstances and being at ease with those decisions. After all, investing should be enjoyable.

It's never easy to put your hard-earned dollars into something with no guarantee, but sensible investment based on thorough research and taking calculated risks can lead to good rewards. But remember, investing is a journey – you will have ups and downs. If it sounds too good to be true, it probably is. One of the largest Ponzi schemes in recent history involved Bernie Madoff, a Wall Street financier and investor, who promised his clients consistent and positive returns every single year, even when the market was down. He managed to embezzle $65 billion US dollars over the years.

Here's a graph to demonstrate different asset types with potential return and risk. Conservative investors may prefer a larger proportion towards the left to seek stability, while those with a higher risk appetite may look to the right-hand side. Of course, this is only an illustrative diagram; there are variations even within each asset type.

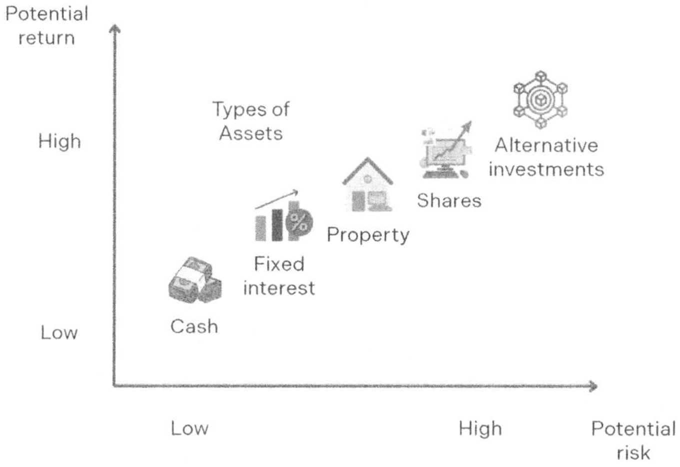

In it for the long haul

You can make some extraordinary profit with speculative investing, and on the other side of the coin, extraordinary loss. For most of us investing in our financial future, the 'boring and stress-free' approach might be preferable, with a focus on a steady and long-term investment strategy. Time can often do the heavy lifting when it comes to growth. While it doesn't sound very glamorous, there is definitely a compelling case to be made for stability and consistency over time.

We can see this play out in the real world. Let's take a look at the NASDAQ Composite:

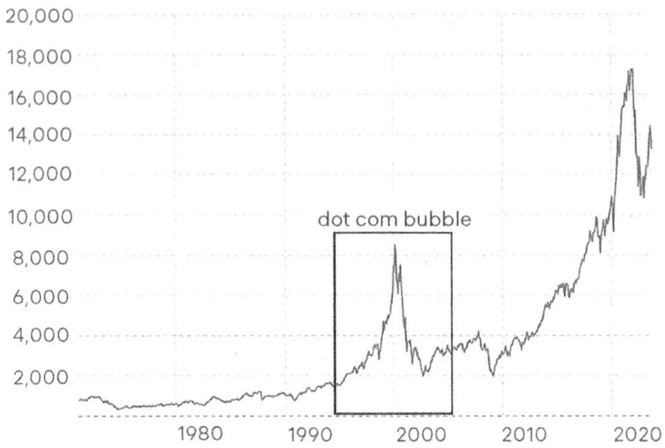

Figure 4: *NASDAQ Composite over the last 40 years*[20]

NASDAQ Composite is an index that represents the performance of many companies listed on the NASDAQ stock exchange in the United States. It is often used as a benchmark for internet, telecommunication and technology sectors.

You may have heard of the dot-com bubble that occurred from the mid-1990s to early 2000s. It was the start of the internet and the world wide web was taking off. Many investors were in a frenzy about the potential. Even companies that had no revenue still had high valuations and stocks were overvalued. As long as you had a .com in your name, people were prepared to throw money at you because it was the era of new technology and the internet, and they were the future! But the good times didn't last and the value plummeted. The bubble burst at the start of the 2000s, set off by rising interest rates and closer scrutiny over the actual financial performance of many of the companies. It was estimated $5 trillion was lost. It was one of the most famous speculative bubbles in investment history.

The story doesn't end there though – fast forward to where we are today. The NASDAQ Composite has not only recovered but soared well past its previous peak. This is the power of long-term investing.

Let's explore some asset classes in more detail so you can gain an understanding of how they can contribute to building a diverse and balanced investment portfolio in the long term for you.

Stocks

Stock explained simply

STOCKS AND SHARES – WHAT'S THE DIFFERENCE?

Stocks are basically pieces of a company you can buy. When you buy stock of a specific company, you own a part of that company. Shares represent a single unit of a stock. But these terms are often used interchangeably.

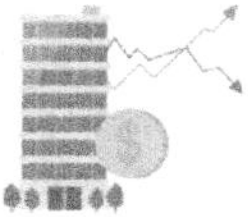

Stocks represent ownership in a company

The value of a stock can go up or down based on the company's performance and investor perception

The stock market is a marketplace for investors to buy and sell company's shares

Companies issue stocks to raise money from investors

When you buy a stock, you become a partial owner of the company

As a shareholder, you have voting rights and may receive dividends

Let's look at an example:

Helen loves cooking and experimenting with food. She has come up with a great way to make ice cream – ice crystals never form and the flavours are out of this world. It's always a big hit at family gatherings and parties with friends. Everyone raves about how great the ice cream tastes.

This sparks an idea – why not turn her delicious idea into a business? She forms a business plan and approaches her network of friends and family to pitch her idea. Eager to be part of her adventure, they invest money into her business. In exchange, she provides them with ownership shares of the company. They are now shareholders of Helen's private company. Through this undertaking, she manages to raise enough funds to set up a store in one of the popular spots right by Bondi Beach in Sydney.

As the word spreads, Helen's ice cream store takes off. She is featured in *Time Out* and the *Good Food Guide*, and now there's always a queue outside the store. Her social media is bombarded with people asking when she plans to open up a store near them. To keep up with demand and to reach even more customers, she expands. Helen gets finance through bank loans, re-invests some of the profit, and her family and friends invest more money. Over the next couple of years, she has stores in all major cities in Australia.

This gives Helen the confidence boost for even grander aspirations. She wants to take her ice cream to even more places and maybe even outside Australia. The amount of funding required means she has to go beyond her existing network and ways of raising funds. She decides to take her company public. This means she can now offer shares of her ice cream empire to the public. Helen goes through the process of an initial public offering (IPO) which takes a private company into a public one.

She enlists the help of legal experts and investment bankers to determine the value of her business and sets the price for the shares that will be offered, as part of getting ready for her company's IPO. It's a lot of hard work but Helen perseveres and completes all the necessary processes. She can't wait for more people to enjoy her ice cream. On IPO day, her business is officially listed on the stock exchange. Now investors can buy shares in Helen's amazing ice cream business.

And many investors do buy shares. They have all heard about the amazing taste of her ice cream and believe in her business expansion plans. With the funds raised, her business grows exponentially. She has also used the money to innovate even more and now has an entire range of ice cream cakes and delicacies, not to mention introducing efficiencies in equipment and staff to create ice cream in half the time.

Her ice cream business is doing amazingly well; so is the value of the shares. It's a win-win for Helen and her shareholders. In fact, she does so well that she decides to share some of the company profit with her shareholders through dividends. After all, they invested in her company and have helped it to be the success it is today.

This is how Helen took her great talent of making ice cream to a successful public company that's going to take over the ice cream world.

How can you invest money into Helen's ice cream business?

Once an IPO happens, public companies like Helen's ice cream business make their company shares available for trading on the stock exchange. Some of the biggest stock exchanges in the world are the New York Stock Exchange (NYSE), National Association of Securities Dealers Automated Quotations (NASDAQ), Shanghai Stock Exchange (SEE), Euronext and Japan Stock Exchange (JPX). There are three in Australia: the Australian Securities Exchange (ASX), National Stock Exchange (NSX) and Cboe Australia (CXA).

ASX is the biggest exchange in Australia, and there are over 2000 companies listed. Companies trading on ASX usually have three-letter codes that act as unique identifiers for each company. For example, ASX:CBA is Commonwealth Bank of Australia. This makes it easy to find and track the stocks. The prices are dynamic and constantly changing as there is buying and selling throughout the trading day. The prices that get flashed up on the news or financial websites are usually what the last price paid for it was during the day.

Getting started

You need a broker to buy and sell shares on the stock exchange. A broker is the middleman that helps you to place your orders and connects you to the stock exchange. There are two main options – full-service brokers and online trading platforms.

- *Full service:* these are firms that provide investment services and advice. They usually have a team of financial advisors that help investors with various aspects of investing. They may help you to do research, planning and recommend specific strategies. In case of stocks, they may recommend specific shares for you to purchase. They usually charge you a percentage of the total value of a trade.

- *Online trading platforms* are web-based platforms where you can choose what shares to buy and sell yourself. The fees are generally lower as you are making the purchases by yourself. There are quite a few options available, so check the fees and features available to choose the right one. Some names to get you started: Commsec, eToro, GO Markets, Pearler.

A good place to start if you are planning to buy stocks is to open a trading account with your preferred broker. If you want to have some professional help and more guidance, consider a full-service broker. If you are happy to do your own research and are comfortable purchasing, online brokerage might be the way to go.

Then, it's all about choosing the companies you want to invest in. If you don't know what specific companies you are interested in, here are some thought prompters to get you going:

- Are there particular sectors or industries you're familiar with and interested in?
- What is the economy doing? Think from a global, country and even local perspective, and how might that influence certain companies or industries.
- Are there any emerging trends? Pay attention to market trends and economic cycles.
- Jump online and hunt for resources – analyst reports, financial news and websites.

Use the information to narrow down the companies you are interested in, then keep digging and continue doing more research about the specific companies: their long-term strategy, their business outlook, their profit and loss. Their investor annual report is usually a great place to source this information.

If you are going to buy shares of a company, then you are a part owner of that company. As a potential part owner of the company, you want to make sure the company is worth investing in.

Once you are happy with the information you have gathered, it's time to place an order to become a shareholder of the company or companies you have chosen. Consider how much you are willing to spend on the purchase and don't go overboard. One of my old mentors always said: 'Invest all the money you can afford to lose.'

MORE **JARGON** YOU MAY HEAR ARE THE TERMS **SHORT** AND **LONG**:

A *long* position is when you own a stock and expect the stock will increase in value in the future.

A *short* position is basically a bet that the stock price will decrease in the future. You borrow the stock from the broker and sell it to the market at the current value, repurchase it at a lower price, return the stock to the broker and keep the profit.

There are two main types of buy and sell stock orders:

- A *limit order* is typically when you want to buy or sell shares at a specific price. If you are buying, then you can set a maximum price that you are willing to pay. For example, you might want to buy this bag of chocolate, but only if it's $2. If the share price becomes available at that price during the timeframe you set, voilà!
- A *market order* is typically when you accept the market price of the share at the time of buying so you can buy it immediately. For example, you might want to buy a bag of chocolate today and you don't care how much it costs, as long as you get your chocolate fix right now.
- Once your trade order goes through, you have to transfer money into your trading account to cover the cost of the order and the transaction fee. The settlement period for ASX

is usually two business days, so make sure you give yourself plenty of time to transfer the money so you don't get a late penalty fee.

- Depending on the number of shares you buy, your voice in company matters will vary. If you own a significant portion, you will have more voting power in their decisions, like electing the board of directors. Although it is more likely for most investors to hold a relatively small percentage of ownership, sometimes a fraction of a percent.
- Once you are the proud owner of shares, don't forget to keep an eye on the performance of your company, but try not to look at the price every day. As humans, we tend to be biased toward loss aversion, so we feel the pain of a loss more strongly than the satisfaction of a gain. Studies have shown that when we look at the charts on a daily basis, we tend to get absorbed by the short-term fluctuations. If we get absorbed by short-term trends, we may become a little too enthusiastic about buying or selling and forget about our long-term plan. Fluctuations are just a natural part of the share market.
- If you have done your research thoroughly, trust yourself. Remember, we are investors, not traders, so we have to exhibit smart investing behaviour.

Dividends

Depending on your investment goals, you may want to have a continuous income stream from your shares. This is where dividends come in. Dividends are paid by certain companies to their shareholders as a way to reward them. Instead of keeping all the profit, the company shares this with its investors.

There are franked and unfranked dividends:

Franked dividends are where the company already paid taxes on the profits they used to give dividends. This means you don't need to pay taxes on those dividends again when you add them in your total income.

Unfranked dividends are the opposite. The company hasn't paid taxes on the profit and you will need to pay taxes on that money when you include it as part of your total income at tax return time.

How does the stock market keep track of my shares?

When you buy shares of any ASX public listed company, a record is created and maintained by ASX's settlement and clearing system known as CHESS – the Clearing House Electronic Subregister System. During the purchase, your broker facilitates and registers the ownership in your name within the CHESS system. Each investor has a unique Holder Identification (HIN) and this is the identifier for our holdings. This process ensures your ownership is securely recorded and tracked.

Share registry companies such as ComputerShare and Link Market Services are share registry providers for a big chunk of ASX listed companies. They handle the listed company's share registry and related administrative services, such as maintaining shareholders records, distributing dividends, etc. They work in conjunction with CHESS to manage the share ownership of the listed companies.

Look beyond our shores

Looking at ASX listed companies can be a good start to your stock investing journey, but don't limit yourself to it. Once you're ready, you could consider opportunities beyond our borders. The Australian share market only represents 2% of global stock markets. By investing your funds internationally, you are expanding your investing horizons to gain a much larger range of industries and companies around the world. We know that diversification is a smart idea as it spreads risk across different regions and economies, not to mention avoiding being overly influenced by the performance of companies listed only in Australia.

Managed funds (including index funds)

When I listen to music, I usually like to pick a playlist instead of selecting individual artists or playing the same songs over and over. That's the same way I look at managed funds.

Imagine a song is like a company listed on the stock exchange. Just as songs belong to different genres such as pop or reggae, companies belong to specific sectors, like healthcare or technology. A managed fund may contain a playlist for a particular genre, or if you really want to shake things up, a mixture of genres, artists and songs.

In this playlist, you will find a collection of the 'best of' songs, just as a managed fund has selected investments that share a common theme. You don't have to do the hard work of choosing; you can just opt for the playlist. Larger companies will have more of an impact on the playlist, the same as more songs are played from a popular artist than a less popular one.

If you don't want to listen to a single song (i.e. invest in a single company), a playlist can be a better choice. Just like a playlist, managed funds offer diversification by including different investments with a similar theme. Who doesn't love a greatest hits list?

You may hear managed funds getting referred to by the American term *mutual funds*. They are basically the same but with some very subtle differences. But let's focus on managed funds for now. Managed funds are a type of investment where you pool your money together with other people. The investment contains assets that can be a mixture of shares, cash, bonds, etc. You, as an investor, would own units of the managed fund. When the investments in the fund increase or decrease in value, the value of your units also change. You can buy and sell managed funds units, and the price is determined by the end of the trading day based on the total of the fund's assets. This price is called the Net Asset Value (NAV).

There are many types of managed funds available, ranging from single assets to mixed assets in their portfolio. Some may only have shares; others may have a range of shares and properties. All with its own unique strategy, asset allocation plan and fee structure.

There are active and passive investment approaches:

- *Active managed funds* are where fund managers are actively selecting investments for the fund and they are trying to generate a higher return than a particular benchmark or index. They are like specialist DJs curating a playlist. The portfolio is adjusted over time so fund managers can capitalise on opportunities or respond to changing conditions in the economy. Because there's a lot of effort involved, there is usually a higher fee associated with this type of fund.

- *Passive managed funds* usually track a benchmark or index. It is a more hands-off approach. Instead of trying to outperform the market, they aim to copy the performance of a specific index or benchmark. They also try to copy the exact structure and returns of the specific index by holding the same allocation of

This is also known as index funds

assets. For example, the ASX200 index is representing the performance of the top 200 companies listed on the ASX. These companies come from many different sectors like industrial, resources, financials, healthcare and more. The ASX200 is like the Top 200 hottest, top-played songs in Australia! The good thing about index funds is that if one or two companies don't do well, others are going to prop up the bad performers. There is no frequent trading or extensive research involved, hence the lower management fees compared to active funds.

The 'active' approach may appeal to some of us more – you may want to have an expert picking and choosing assets and seek the potential of higher returns. Some of us might prefer the 'passive' approach and trust that market-average returns will win out in the long run. The famous investor Warren Buffet recommends index funds in his investment advice. He also puts his money where his mouth is. In 2008, he made a cool $1 million dollar bet with a hedge-fund manager that a low-cost S&P500 index fund would outperform actively managed hedge funds over a ten-year period. You know what? He won the bet.

To buy managed funds – you need to have a trading account, do your research of what you would like to invest in, and place your order. All Australian managed funds provide a PDF that outlines the fund's strategy, risks, fees and other relevant information. Don't forget to take a closer look before going ahead with the purchase. If you are looking at a popular managed fund, like a fund that is tracking the ASX200 index, compare the management fees to other funds tracking the same thing – you might as well pay less fees if you can!

Exchange-traded funds (ETFs)

ETFs are the newest kid on the block – since the '90s anyway. ETFs are similar to managed funds, except you can trade them like shares on a stock exchange. The most common ETFs track an index. Same as managed funds, you buy units of the ETF itself and not the individual investments it holds. The company that manages the ETF owns those investments. The fees for ETFs are relatively low and can provide diversification to your portfolio with a range of assets. Once again, they are a great option without the need to purchase individual assets.

The number of ETF units can change depending on demand, i.e. how many people want to buy or sell them. This helps keep the price of the ETF units in close alignment with the total value of all the investments in the ETF (Net Asset Value or NAV).

Let's say you are interested in an ETF that tracks the performance of an index focused on a diversified portfolio of companies providing services and products that address climate change. The NAV of this ETF is $1 per share at the start of the trading day. It holds a portfolio of companies' stocks with a total value of $1,000,000 and there are 1,000,000 shares of the ETF in circulation. Throughout the trading day, investors are buying and selling the ETF on the stock exchange. The United Nations announces its absolute commitment to achieve net zero emissions in five years' time with no further delays. This increases demand for all companies in the sustainability sector, including demand for the ETF during the day. Due to this increased demand, the ETF price increases to $1.20 per share. The NAV remains the same at $1. Since the market price exceeds NAV, specialised fund managers (authorised participants) can create new shares and sell them on the market. By the end of the trading day, the market price should be closer to the NAV of the ETF.

Quick summary

Here's a summary to make it easier to compare managed funds, index funds and ETFs:

	Active managed funds	**Index funds (passive managed funds)**	**Exchange-traded funds**
Diversified investments	✓	✓	✓
Strategy	Professionally managed portfolio	Following a benchmark index	Track an underlying asset, but most commonly an index
Performance goal	Outperform the market	Match benchmark	Match benchmark
Fund approach	Active	Passive	Passive (mostly)
Management fees	High	Low	Low
Traded on stock exchange	✕	✕	✓
Pricing	Once per day	Once per day	Changes throughout the day

P.S. If managed funds, index funds and ETFs invest in companies that pay dividends, then you will get them passed on to you at the end of each distribution period. One thing to note, the fund itself does not pay tax on the distributions; it's up to you to include them as part of your taxable income.

Commodities

Commodity trading can sound mysterious and complex, but it is one of the earliest investment types in history. A commodity, according to the *Cambridge Dictionary*, is a substance or product that can be traded, bought or sold. In other words, commodities are the raw goods or materials we use every day:

- Livestock and meat – including goods such as beef and milk
- Agricultural – including crops such as wheat, corn, soybeans and sugar

- Energy – including crude oil, natural gas and coal
- Metals – including industrial metals such as copper and precious metals such as gold.

You may also hear them being categorised into 'soft' and 'hard' commodities. The most traded commodities today are crude oil, coffee, natural gas, gold and wheat.

Some investors like commodities because they go up when inflation goes up, protecting your money from losing its buying power. It can be a way to keep your money staying strong even if prices are increasing. Commodities are sometimes seen as risky because it is difficult to predict supply and demand, i.e. how much something is available vs. how much people want it. For example, in agriculture with weather patterns, disasters etc.

There are several common ways to invest in commodities:

- Physically buy it. For example, you might want to buy a gold or silver coin. Speaking of silver trading, there were a couple of brothers in the 1970s who tried to control the world silver market by buying as much of it as possible. The price of silver skyrocketed. The government worried about economic stability and intervened. The price eventually came crashing down and the brothers ended up bankrupt. A cautionary tale of trying to control market forces!

- Buy shares in companies that produce the commodity. But remember the company is more than just the commodity it makes. The share price is not only influenced by the price of the commodity, but also how the company is managed and what is happening in the market.
- ETFs and managed funds. You can invest in a fund that focuses on specific commodities or a group of commodities, indexes or related assets.
- Future contracts. This is where you make a deal today to buy or sell something at a set price on a future date. Sort of like betting on whether the price will go up or down. If you're just starting on your investing journey, then it might be better to start with one of the other ways until you can get a better handle on the commodities market.

A good place to start could be to focus on specific markets you find interesting and want to learn more about. For example, you may be very interested in electric vehicles and you are familiar with the market drivers. This might lead to you reading more about the base metal lithium, which is used in electric vehicle batteries. Countries like Australia, Chile and China are the biggest producers of the metal. Its production and pricing are likely to be influenced by the increasing demand for more environmentally friendly cars and advancements in battery technology. This leads you to do more research around international policies and how they might influence manufacturing and trade, how a trade embargo might influence the pricing and manufacturing of raw materials and finished goods. You may keep an eye on the market trends for electric cars and how might it look in five years. You might investigate alternative vehicle options, like emerging technologies such as hydrogen fuel for hydrogen cars. And so on and so on ... you can see there are many considerations. The more you understand the market dynamics, the more aware you will become of the risks and benefits, and the better equipped you are to make the right investment choices.

Bonds

Did you know that over half of the debt in the global economy is made up of bonds?

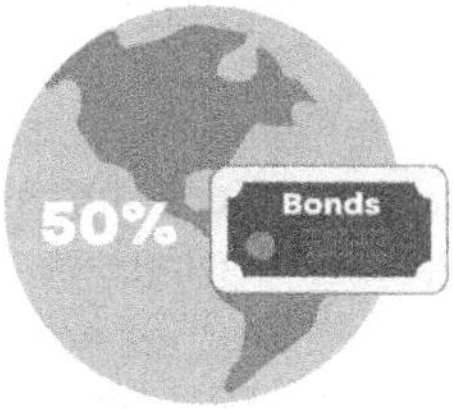

Bonds are like a loan. They are debt securities issued by companies or governments. When you buy a bond, you are lending money to the issuer (company or government). In return, they will pay you back the amount you lent (the *principal*) at a specific date (*maturity date*), which can range from months to years. During the duration of the loan, the issuer will pay you interest (*coupon*). There are three main types:

- **Fixed rate:** the coupon rate remains the same throughout the life of the loan period. This means you will know exactly how much you will get paid until the maturity date. This is the most common.
- **Floating rate:** the coupon rate is tied to a benchmark, such as the Bank Bill Swap Rate or 90-day Bank Bill Swap Rate. This means the coupon payments will increase if the interest rates go up, and by the same token, decrease if the interest rates go down.

- **Indexed:** the principal value and coupon rate is adjusted based on the consumer price index (CPI) changes. As the CPI rises, the bond's principal value and coupon increase, offering you protection against inflation.

> **CPI – CONSUMER PRICE INDEX**
> Is a way to measure how the price of everyday things we buy change over time. It helps us to look at the cost of living, and the government uses the CPI to monitor inflation.

Bonds are usually considered to be one of the less riskier investment options. This is because they offer a fixed income stream and the issuer has a legal obligation to return the borrowed money at the maturity date.

Government bonds are usually considered to be safest as they have the government's backing while company bonds depend on the financial health of the company. Corporate bonds usually require large amounts of money to be invested and are usually not publicly traded (there are exceptions though), so you will have to go through a broker to access this. Managed funds for bonds are also an option.

If you are interested in Australian government bonds, the easiest way may be to look at the exchanged-traded bonds on the ASX. In Australia, there are Australian Government Bonds (AGB, also known as *treasury bonds*) and semi-government bonds which are issued by states and territories. There are two main types – exchange-traded treasury bonds (eTBs) and exchange-traded treasury indexed bonds (eTIBs). eTBs provide fixed rate payment every six months and can be traded on ASX. eTIBs adjust their payment based on CPI (i.e. indexed) and provide payment every three months. Bond prices do fluctuate depending on market conditions and interest rates.

Options

Picture this, you are about to head out to an outdoor festival because Beyoncé is playing. The weather is looking good; you have a great group of friends going; it's going to be a great gig. Because of the rather unpredictable weather in the last few weeks, the festival is offering party-goers a chance to buy a raincoat before the day –pay $5 for the right to buy the raincoat at $10 at the festival. This option gives you the right to buy a raincoat at $10, but there is no obligation to buy it. For peace of mind that bad weather won't be a reason for missing the festival, you pay the $5.

It ends up raining on the day, the price of the raincoat at the festival goes up to $20 because of the high demand. Since you already have the raincoat option, you use it and buy a raincoat at $10 as the agreed price, even though they are selling them to everyone else at $20. However, if it doesn't rain or you don't want a raincoat, you can choose to let that option expire. Although, bear in mind, you lose the $5 you used to buy it in the first place.

That's pretty much how options work.

Options, or exchange-traded options, are contracts that give you the right, but not the obligation to buy or sell an asset, such as shares, at a specific price (*exercise* or *strike price*) on or before a specific date (*expiration date*). For you, our Beyoncé goer, the exercise price was the $5 and the expiration date was the festival date.

Options can cover different types of assets such as bonds, ETFs, shares and indexes. There are two ways to trade options:

- A **call option** gives you the right to buy an asset at the exercise price before or on the expiration date. This is typically used when you expect the price of the asset to increase.
- A **put option** gives you the right to sell an asset at the price before or on the expiration date. This is typically used when you expect the price to decrease.

Options trading is about being able to predict the price of the asset and see what happens next. When the price of the asset changes, it will also change the option's value, so you can make a profit by trading it. Let's go back to the festival for a second. During the festival, it starts pouring down with rain and the option suddenly becomes a lot more valuable than the $5 that you paid. You can sell this for a profit to others, or you can buy the raincoat at $10 and sell it at $20. You basically turned your $5 into more money. So imagine how many more raincoat options you might have bought if you were able to predict the weather accurately all the time!

Options trading can be more affordable and profitable as you start with a smaller amount of money paid upfront. But if you are quite new to investing, starting with options trading can be rather challenging, as it is more complex than other investment options. So before you dive in, it's a good idea to gain a deeper understanding of what you are investing in because it's about predicting what's to come.

Cryptocurrency

Cryptocurrency (crypto) has been around for a few years and many millions have been earned and lost during this time. Investing in crypto can be seen as speculative investing, with potential high reward but high risk. What exactly is cryptocurrency? Let's start with a quick introduction.

In the traditional world, aka non-blockchain world, governments and banks act as the authorities that keep ledgers and records of transactions and data. We trust these banks and our government to manage the financial and personal information in an accurate and secure way.

Then blockchain came along.

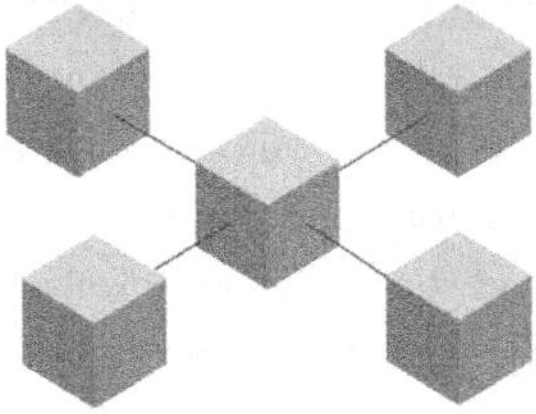

Blockchain is basically a ledger to keep track of transactions in the digital world. A transaction is an exchange of something, like receiving or sending money.

For example, instead of raining at the outdoor festival, it was super sunny. Your friend Anna buys a pair of sunglasses. Instead of getting a paper receipt, her purchase is recorded on a digital block. This digital block contains all the data from the transaction, like where she bought the glasses, how much they cost, etc. This record is written with a digital permanent marker, so it can't be easily changed or erased. It also has an unbreakable lock that only the correct key can open.

Before it can get be included in the public ledger, the transaction must be verified. The details are sent to a network of independent auditors. These auditors go through the information in great detail, making sure the transaction is valid and follows the system rules. If there is unanimous agreement from all the auditors, this block is added to a chain of other blocks and a blockchain is created. Once the block is part of the chain, the transaction is now complete and final.

Since the blockchain is a ledger that contains a record of all the previous transactions in the system, and everyone on the network can see the ledger, this makes blockchain very transparent. Any changes will need consensus from everyone on the network, making it very difficult to change anything without people noticing.

Unlike the conventional world, blockchain is decentralised, so it's not a single person or a central authority in charge. Everyone works together to make sure everything is kept in balance; everyone has the same information and decisions are made collectively. No wonder people (and government) are nervous, scared and excited about this technology!

You can put all sorts of data and information on blockchain – cryptocurrency is just one type. There are many cryptocurrencies available; some of the popular ones include Bitcoin, Ethereum and Tether.

> If you are tech savvy, you might even want to try mining for cryptocurrency. Mining is basically where computers solve problems to add transaction data to the global public ledger of previous transactions; the part of verifying transactions is called mining. When you do this, you get rewarded with coins. It sounds easy, but you will need to have special computer equipment and it uses a HUGE amount of electricity. You can get much smarter on this topic on the almighty internet.

Cryptocurrency is a currency and investment. You can use cryptocurrency to make purchases as an alternative to traditional currencies. Have you heard the story about the computer programmer who used 10,000 bitcoins onto buy two pizzas? They were only worth $41 at that time, but they are definitely the most expensive pizzas ever bought today! There are many countries that allow the use of these digital currencies, although it is illegal in some countries. In Australia, the Australian Tax Office treats Bitcoin as an asset that can be taxed in certain situations, like buying/selling/using Bitcoin. Don't forget to keep a record of all your transactions as you are may have to pay capital gains tax.

Many people buy cryptocurrency expecting the value to increase over time. The crypto market is incredibly volatile, and most investors are likely to experience some rollercoaster rides in a short timeframe. So a few things to note:

- There is a lack of international regulations. Cryptocurrency operates outside traditional financial systems, so it's not regulated by governments or central banks. Since there are no clear guidelines, this can lead to price manipulation and price swings.
- There is a strong dependency on investor speculation and sentiment. Crypto is such a hot topic and it attracts a lot of investors looking for a quick profit. Public sentiment, news and even rumours can have a significant impact on pricing. For example, on 29 January 2021, Elon Musk added #bitcoin to his X (Twitter) bio. The Bitcoin price increased from $32,000 to $38,000 in just a few hours.
- Crypto is still new and shiny. Because it's so new and not that many currencies exist, it means changes can lead to big fluctuations in the entire crypto market.
- There is no real value. Cryptocurrency is not like a company that earns money or owns real estate; its value depends on how much people want it or find it useful. The more people want it, the more the value increases, and if nobody wants it, the value drops. There are no assets or earnings to back up the cryptocurrency.

Wise investment gurus say: 'Only invest in things that you understand.' Consider living by this rule for all investing, but it's especially true for cryptocurrency. We are only at the beginning and there will be much more technological advancement still to come. The potential risk and potential rewards are high. If crypto is something you are considering, do your research so you understand the market dynamics.

NFTs

We can't discuss cryptocurrency and not mention NFTs. NFTs took the world by storm when memes, Bored Apes or even the first-ever tweet became highly sought after and bought for crazy amounts of money. How much they are worth today is a different story.

NFTs, otherwise known as non-fungible tokens, are built on blockchain technology. They are digital assets that show who owns something unique, such as artworks or videos. They prove the item's authenticity and ownership on the internet. I like to think of NFTs as ownership certificates for digital items. If you own an NFT for a particular GIF, then you have the official record of ownership for that GIF on the blockchain. It doesn't mean you have physical possession, but you are the exclusive owner in the digital world.

Cryptocurrency like Bitcoin or the Australian dollar are fungible, so every unit is the same value as another unit. NFTs are not. Each token is unique so they can't be exchanged on a one-to-one basis. This uniqueness is what gives NFTs their value and appeal. The value of NFTs is determined by various factors, such as who was the creator, how rare it is, how popular it is, and how much hype there is. Similar to a lot of artworks today, really! Who determines that a Picasso painting is worth more than a painting done by you? It's subjective and all to do with tastes and preferences.

But how do people, in particular people like us, make money from NFTs? Here are two common ways:

- Buy and sell. Similar to other investments, like shares, we all want to buy low and sell it for a profit when the value increases. NFTs, perhaps even more than cryptocurrency, have no real value because there is no underlying asset and the pricing is completely dependent on demand. Some collectors invest in rare or unique digital items as only a few copies have been 'minted' and they believe this will have more demand.

- Create and sell. Theoretically almost anyone can mint their digital work and sell it. Many artists, content creators and musicians mint their work as NFTs and sell them. Beeple, aka Mike Winkelmann, catapulted NFTs into the mainstream when he sold a piece of crypto-art for $69 million dollars in 2021.
- While NFTs may have lost their popularity, it is definitely a new way of possessing things. There is no doubt that many in the industry are looking at the potential ways that NFTs may transform aspects of our lives. With the world sprinting towards technology advances like blockchain and generative artificial intelligence, we all have a role to play in understanding and re-thinking how we interact and perceive ownership in the digital age.

Real estate

Australians love property. Probably more than any other nation in the world. The Australian property market is valued at $9.7 trillion dollars in 2023.[21] To put this into context – the Sydney Opera House, the most famous building in Australia – cost $102 million dollars to build, so that's a total of 98,039 Sydney Opera Houses!

Real estate is part of the Australian dream and is deeply ingrained in our culture. There are constant news articles about the real estate market and TV shows dedicated to home renovations; people talk about it over barbeques. It's true. We love property, and we are not afraid to show it.

Based on the 2021 Australian Bureau of Statistics census data, more females were owner-occupiers than males, with 55% of homes either solely or jointly owned by women compared to 52% by men. This is a rather encouraging statistic! But it's not quite the same for investment properties as discussed earlier in the chapter.

Whether you want to find a place to call home or are looking to invest, it can be daunting but the rewards can outweigh the apprehension. There are many types of properties that could be suitable for your needs – apartments, units/villas, freestanding houses, house and land packages, commercial... the list goes on. There are idiosyncrasies with each of these assets, and it's important that you do your homework before jumping into the purchase. Sometimes when we talk about something so much, we fool ourselves into thinking we know more than we do.

Real estate is considered a relatively safe and long-term asset. Of course, there are peaks and falls like there are with any other type of investment. The performance can vary between property type, geographical locations such as capital cities or regional areas, and even down to suburb and street level. The graph below shows the median house value by capital city, which gives you a glimpse of market performance over the last few decades. At a higher level, the real estate market has been increasing by an average of 5.4% per year for the last 30 years.

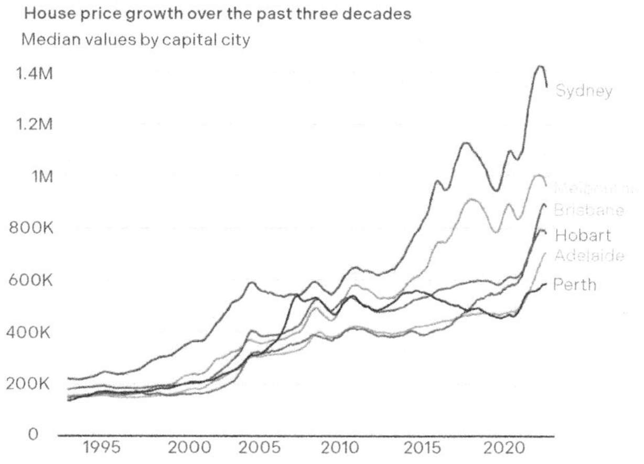

Figure 6: *source – CoreLogic*

There are many speculators saying that the Australian real estate market is in a bubble, but it is incredibly difficult to know what lies ahead. There are so many market drivers that determine the value – interest rates, macro- and micro-economic activities, immigration, etc. But what we can look at is what the real estate market has been doing until now, and how to navigate this major investment.

Even if you are not buying a mansion by the harbour, buying a property is still undeniably one of the largest purchases a person is likely to make in their life. Since this is such a major purchase and we do it so infrequently, it would be wise to plan out some key things you might want to think about, research and action.

My journey into the world of property had a pretty rocky start. I was living in New Zealand at the time, feeling the pressure to buy a home due to FOMO and societal expectations. This was during the infamous 'leaky home' crisis, where poorly constructed houses were plagued by water leaks, moisture issues and structural troubles. Since insurance and warranties didn't cover the damage, homeowners were left with hefty repair bills. We were a little wary, since that's what we were hearing on the daily news, but still wanted to jump on the bandwagon – after all, 'everyone else' was doing it.

It all started well. We secured conditional pre-approval from the bank for a purchase price we were comfortable with. We didn't have any firm criteria and just wanted something within our price range, so we explored a few properties in a few different areas. Much of the time, the advertised prices were significantly lower than the actual selling prices. Unfortunately, this under-quoting practice still goes on today.

After a few weeks, we stumbled upon a rather lovely house in a sought-after neighbourhood. It had a backyard and was on a quiet street right next to a blue-chip suburb. We went to see it before its upcoming auction even though we knew it was beyond our reach, just a quick tour to get a feel of what sort of place you could get in the area.

I have never been to an auction before; I wanted to use this house as a test case to observe and learn the process involved. A few days later, auction day arrived during my lunch break. Standing amidst a small crowd outside the house, my partner and I watched the action unfold. The bidding started slow – the selling agent was in his element, talking to people individually to rally up the bidding.

And it worked ... because the next thing I knew, my partner raised his hand to bid, catching me off guard. What happened next was really a blur because we were just there to watch! To cut a long story short, we ended up winning the auction.

Sounds like good news, right? Not exactly. We quickly found out that an auction means it's an unconditional sale and you have to buy the house as is. We had spent a total of 10 minutes at the house – and that's being generous. No lawyer had reviewed the contract; we didn't conduct any building inspections to check the house's quality; and we didn't even have the deposit ready – which we had 24 hours to produce. Needless to say, we were totally clueless.

The rest of the day was manic. I went back to work but didn't get much work done. I spoke to the broker who immediately spoke to the bank and got the ball rolling. I managed to grab a solicitor's details from a friend for the contract. The cherry on the cake was, when I was frantically scrambling money from various accounts and sources including a travel credit card that had been untouched since the start of the year, I discovered I'd fallen victim to credit fraud, with $5000 stolen from that account.

Side note, our broker was great. He didn't want to send me into a panic when we first told him about the purchase, as I think he could sense we were stressed enough. However, he had had some clients who had just purchased a similar house to the one we bought, and they were not successful in getting a mortgage due to the construction and the risk of it being a leaky home. Suffice to say, they lost their deposit.

Honestly, the universe must have been watching out for me because things eventually fell into place, rather chaotically. I managed to get the deposit together. The broker gave me the good news that the bank came through with unconditional approval. The contract was rather straightforward, since it was an unconditional sale. Settlement went ahead and we became homeowners!

Sadly, we didn't live at the house for very long before the relationship ended. I got to try my hand at selling the property. The market was hot, and I figured I could do it myself. And sell it I did – for a profit and there was no capital gains tax or agent commission fees. The silver lining of the story.

This marked my first eventful entry into the property market.

I have made almost every mistake possible with this purchase. There was no plan. We just wanted to buy a place. We didn't do enough research; we only picked areas that were close to where we were already living. We had nobody to help, apart from a broker for the loan. I could continue with the many mistakes, but it might take a while to list them all! To sum it up – we did no due diligence. It all worked out in the end, but it was just pure dumb luck.

I hope you can learn from my mistakes and they serve as a reminder of the importance of planning, knowledge and preparation when it comes to such significant investments. Since that initial rollercoaster ride, I now have a property portfolio. Mistakes (or unexpected surprises) still happen, but now they are smaller, less risky and managed when they happen. My property journey has been marked by ups and downs, but it's been a lot smoother sailing than that could-have-been disastrous first start.

I believe property is a great investment vehicle for building wealth, so I want to spend some time discussing the different steps and what's involved.

Let's get into it!

Do you want a home or investment property?

This question can act as a great starting point in guiding you to determine the type of property you will buy and how you might get started. Some things to consider:

- Why do you want to buy a property? Is it a place to create memories? Or is it a vehicle for financial gains to expand your investment portfolio?
- Where are you in life? Are you fairly settled and planning to live in one place for quite a few years to come?
- Are you ready for the responsibilities of owning a house or an investment property? Both come with a different set of responsibilities, such as paying council and water rates, fixing property issues and maintaining the property.
- Are you looking for more regular income to supplement your income as part of your financial goals?

If you're looking for a place for a place to call home, then what neighbourhoods do you like that you can afford to live in? Perhaps you can't afford to live where you really want to, but you still want to get on the property ladder, so could you consider rent-vesting as an option?

If you are thinking about an investment property, are you comfortable with the risks of the real estate market? Having an investment property is like running a small business; are you willing to take on the responsibilities of managing finances and income?

Here's a short pros and cons list that looks at the different options for you to consider:

	Owning the property you live in	Owning an investment property and renting where you live	Renting
Pros	• It's your home – you can put nails on the walls and have the freedom to make the property your own. • No rent and paying off your own mortgage. • Potential increase in house value over time and you can use **equity*** to invest in more properties. • More government support via first home owner grant and shared equity schemes. • No capital gains tax when you sell the property.	• You're able to live where you want (owning a property where you want to live is not always possible or affordable) while being on the property ladder. • Rental income pays a portion or all your mortgage. • You may be able to claim deductions for tax benefits. • Diversification in your investment portfolio. • Potential increase in house value over time and you can use equity to invest further.	• Flexibility and freedom to live where you want and leave when you want (lease dependent!). • Landlord pays for your repair and maintenance. • Only have to pay for rent and utilities with no other fees like strata or council rates. • Upfront bond money is minimal compared with house deposit.

Equity – the difference between the current value of your property and the amount left on your loan.

Equity = current value –mortgage debt

This is likely to grow over time as you reduce your loan amount and when the property increases in value. You can borrow against the equity in your property to buy more properties or fund a renovation.

	Owning the property you live in	Owning an investment property and renting where you live	Renting
Cons	• Large upfront costs. • You're tied to a specific location. • There's may be ongoing repair and maintenance costs. • You can't claim expenses as tax deductions. • Limited income potential.	• Large upfront costs. • You have landlord responsibilities like paying for rates, repair and maintenance. • You may have to pay land tax. • You're still at the whim of your landlord where you live. • You're liable for capital gains tax when you sell the property.	• Your rent is paying off someone else's mortgage. • You could be asked to move if the landlord wants to move back or sell the property. • Limited flexibility in personalising where you live. • You can't build equity. • It's harder to find a property that allows pets, although this is changing.

Gather your experts

Whether it's your first or tenth house, a team of trusted advisors is going to make your life so much easier. As soon as you are ready, make a start on researching who they might be. Here are some suggested professionals you could speak to:

- Mortgage broker

  > There are over 100 mortgage lenders in Australia..

  They will help to evaluate your position financially and inform you how lenders would see it. Some people prefer to deal with banks directly because they have been with the same bank for the last 10 years or they contact a few different lenders to try to get the best deal. This is where a mortgage broker can help. Rather than dealing with just one bank, they have access to many more lenders, and they will do all the hard work on your behalf. Brokers should know specific preferences and requirements of different lenders and can help you determine how much you can borrow and discuss what options and lenders would best suit your needs.

- Conveyancer/solicitor

  They will make sure you are covered for all the legal stuff when you are buying or selling a property. For example, looking through the contract and checking terms and conditions, organising title searches, consulting local authorities for anything that may affect the property, and making sure the transaction is legally compliant. Since the rules are different for each state, you need to find a conveyancer who is qualified to operate in the state you are buying from. Solicitors are fully qualified legal experts with extensive knowledge of the law, so they may be better equipped to handle complex sales and issues.

- Buyer agent

  They can act on your behalf to buy a property. These professionals can be a good option if you're inexperienced and/or time poor. From identifying your property goals, to finding you the right property, and handling negotiations right up to property handover, they are your advocate, just as the real estate agent is the seller's advocate. They like to deal with you once you have pre-approval from a lender.

- Accountant

  If you're looking at buying an investment property, it's a good idea to talk to an accountant before the purchase. They can help you with things like structuring, tax rates for calculations and tax planning.

Speaking from my personal experience, having great experts giving you the right advice just makes it so much easier. I have also dealt with some not-so-good ones, which caused many headaches and made it harder and more expensive than it needed to be. Buying property is stressful enough as it is. You want to make the process as smooth as possible by having great people help you along the way. Unless you are doing this every day, it is difficult to remember everything you need to do. These property professionals do this daily, so pick their brains and ask lots of questions. You will learn from their experience to help you do this better.

How can you make sure you are getting the best? Make sure you read the section on 'Your team of experts' under the last chapter in this book.

What's your budget?

This is something the broker can help you with, but it's always a good idea to know your own numbers and what you're comfortable spending before you talk to the broker.

How much do you want to spend on the property? Does this align with how much you can afford? Be realistic. If you earn $60,000 a year, have very little savings and want to buy a $5 million dollar house, it's not realistic to expect you can afford to do it.

Understanding your current budget, covered in 'Second thing – be a budgetista', is a valuable step – how much you have coming in, how much you have going out and how much you have in savings.

You are going to need to have some of this information anyway for your loan application, so it's best to be prepared. Your living costs will likely vary from month to month, so it's best to take the average over a few months. (By the way, if you are in Australia on a temporary or working visa, the process becomes a bit more complicated and more expensive. For example, most lenders may expect a higher deposit from you.)

- **Upfront costs**. This is the amount you are going to have to pay upfront for the house purchase, so you need to have money available and ready.
    - *Deposit.* Most recommend a 20% deposit to avoid paying lenders mortgage insurance (LMI). This insurance is there to protect the lender, not you. There are some lenders that would take a 10% deposit without you incurring LMI, depending on the value of the property. If you happen to be a medical professional, most banks look favourably at you so you can have a less than 20% deposit and avoid LMI.

> Lenders mortgage insurance (LMI) is an one off payment made at settlement, if you are borrowing more than 80% of your home's value. The amount can vary between the size of your deposit and who your lender is.

Nobody likes to pay extra money. However, it is still worthwhile crunching some numbers. Does the benefit of not paying rent or property value increase outweigh the extra money you have to pay for LMI? If it gets you into the market earlier, then it could be a small price to pay compared to the potential of capital growth over the years.

» *Stamp duty*. The amount of stamp duty differs depending on what state the property is in, whether you are a first home buyer, if this is your home or an investment property, and whether it's an existing or off-the-plan property. For example, if you are a first home buyer in Victoria and the property is less than $600,000, then you are exempt from paying stamp duty. As a rough rule of thumb, stamp duty is about 3–4% of the property value.

» *Buffer*. Have a little extra calculated for any unforeseen costs. It will come in handy! For example, if the solicitor fees cost $4000 instead of $2000 like you expected, or when the rates need to be prorated.

Here's a table that can help you in calculating the upfront costs:

Deposit	
Stamp duty	
Legal costs	
Building/pest inspection	
Loan application fee	
Mortgage insurance	
Document preparation fee	
Bank valuation fee	
Title insurance	
Title transfer	
Mortgage registration	
Council/water rates	
Legal searches/enquiries	
Total sum upfront	

- **Ongoing costs**. This is the amount that you will keep paying regularly after the initial purchase. It will help you to determine whether you can manage these expenses on a monthly basis.

Monthly income		Monthly outgoing	
Salary		Mortgage repayments	
Other income (dividends, rent)		Electricity	
		Water	
Income – outgoings =	$	Gas	
		Council and water rates	
		Internet	
		Mobile phone/plan	
		Food/groceries	
		Takeaways/ eating out	
		House- hold supplies	
		Personal/student/ car loan payments	
		Healthcare	
		Education	
		Transport	
		Personal care (clothing, grooming)	

	Building/ contents insurance	
	Health insurance	
	Car insurance	
	Entertainment (streaming services, hobbies, activities)	
	Childcare	
	Other	

Get pre-approved

You will want to have a very good idea of the numbers before you submit your application to a lender. This can be a little trickier for the self-employed, but forward planning with your accountant and broker will make it easier.

Using online calculators does not equate to a proper pre-approval, even if it's on a bank's website. Pre-approval is a formal process from the lenders, which can take between two to three weeks. The pre-approval process gives you a clear understanding of your actual borrowing capacity. Having pre-approval makes it easier to search for properties within your budget; real estate agents will take you more seriously; and it gives you the confidence to act quickly when the right property comes along.

As part of the application, you will need to decide on the ownership type to purchase the property under. Ownership structure is how a property is legally owned, i.e. who has control and rights to the property. This is the name on the title of the property. The most common types are:

- **Sole ownership**: where you are the only owner.

- **Joint tenants**: where you co-own the property with someone else, typically your spouse or partner. Both of you have equal rights to the property.
- **Tenants-in-common**: where you co-own the property with one or more persons. This could be a good option when you are contributing different amounts to others because it divides ownership percentage fairly based on each person's contribution. Though it doesn't automatically cover potential legal issues, you will still need a binding financial agreement to determine how the property will be divided between co-owners.

Other types include trusts, companies and self-managed super funds. You may have heard of people buying properties under these structures. They are not for everyone and they are more complex than buying under your personal name (and potentially more expensive), so make sure you speak to a professional about whether they are right for you.

Once you have the ownership decided, it's time to get ready for some paperwork. Your broker (or bank) will ask you for a whole bunch of documents for the application – payslips, tax returns and proof of identity. Your broker will assess your situation with your specific goals in mind and provide you with recommendations of lenders and options. When you are evaluating these lenders, think about more than just the interest rate. What about other important factors like their customer service, incentives they offer and the overall package they provide?

If the lender you are going with isn't your primary financial institution, you'll need to provide them with evidence of at least three months' worth of transactions. This helps the lender to validate the numbers you've provided in your application and that you didn't understate your expenditure. Make sure you've been on your best spending behaviour in recent months and avoid any big purchase items during this time.

In recent years, banks have tightened their lending criteria and use a more conservative approach to assess an applicant's situation. For example, they may factor in 80% of your income rather than the full 100%, while slightly inflating your expenses. This isn't necessarily a bad thing as it is a move towards more responsible lending and ensures you can manage your repayments comfortably.

An important note: get pre-approval when you are ready to buy and not just for the fun of it; getting multiple pre-approvals can potentially affect your credit score. Also, bear in mind, pre-approvals come with an expiration date, usually a few months.

Feet on the street

If you want to buy a property, hopefully you have already spent time looking at properties online, if not in person already. There are quite a few real estate portals online, realestate.com.au and domain are the most popular search sites real estate agents list properties for sale on. With your pre-approval in hand, it's time to shift gears and get down to business – sourcing the right areas, visiting properties in person and getting a feel for them firsthand.

You don't want to look at everything, everywhere. Narrow it down to the suburbs and the type of property you are interested in. You should spend time, though, looking at properties in the suburbs you like and different streets in the same suburb, as well as nearby suburbs to get a feel for what's in the area. I have spent many hours, weekends and after-hours, attending open houses. Let me tell you, when you have back-to-back house viewings, it's absolute torture to see so many bathrooms when you are in desperate need to go yourself.

The more inspections I attended, the more I developed a sense of properties available and their conditions at different price points. If you are looking at a home to live in, it's even more important to thoroughly check out the neighbourhood and the street.

Real estate agents are pros and they know the importance of presentation. The properties are usually presented beautifully (aka *staging*) – strategically placed furniture, artistically decorated, accent lighting and clutter-free exterior. Staging turns living spaces into inviting homes, makes it easy for you to fall in love with the place and imagine yourself living there. It's all about showcasing the best features, hiding the blemishes to present the property in its best light. Sometimes you can even smell freshly baked cookies! It's all marketing, so don't be swayed by the aesthetics. Look beyond the presentation and assess the property objectively, because you can potentially change all of these things – you can paint a wall to change the colour, buy great furniture – but you can't change the property or the location easily. Here are some questions worth considering:

- Is it big enough for you and your future needs?
- Does the house layout suit you?
- Does the house need renovations and can you handle them?
- What are the nearby amenities?
- If you don't have a car, is public transportation easily accessible?
- What's the local community and environment like?
- What's the noise level like during the day and at night time?
- What's the traffic like during peak hours?
- What's the property like at different hours during the day and after it has rained?

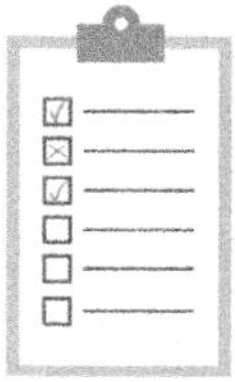

It's a good idea to develop a checklist of your must-haves and deal-breakers to prevent decision fatigue. You don't want to search for months and years chasing a unicorn property. I once knew a couple who sold their house and moved into a granny flat at the back of one of their parents' houses. It was a studio and meant to be a short-term solution until they found a house to buy. But the days turned into weeks and months; they were still living there after the birth of their second child. So get started on that checklist, so you know what you want and work towards that.

Establishing a positive relationship with real estate agents will be super helpful. Agents often handle multiple properties in the same area. Talking to them can provide valuable insights and potentially give you an edge in a competitive market. If you have a good relationship, they may prioritise you as a serious buyer, and you could be the first person they think of when a suitable property comes up for sale. Then you may then get to find out about new listings and inspect the property before others do.

If you have engaged a buyer agent, they would do all of this for you. The buyer agent may already have good relationships with the selling agent and may be more likely to come across off-market deals. These professionals help buyers every day with property purchases. While real estate agents are friendly and make you think you are in your corner, they work for the seller and are aiming to secure the highest price from you. Buyer agents can help you find properties and guide you through the entire buying process. They may also help to reduce the emotions from the buying process, which can help you negotiate the best deal.

Negotiate and make an offer

Once you have found a property you like, it's time to negotiate and make an offer. How you do this depends on the method of sale. The common ways are as follows:

- *Auction* – where potential buyers bid against each other. There is usually a reserve price and the property will only sell once it meets or exceeds that price. The sale is unconditional, which means the highest bidder commits to buying the property without any conditions or negotiations. Some people don't like them, but it's very transparent, as you can see the bidding exactly as the auction goes on.

- *Private treaty* – where the seller determines the price tag to attach to the property for sale. The real estate agent will negotiate with the interested parties to find a willing buyer that either meets or exceeds the listed price. Private treaties come with the option to add in specific terms and the option of a cooling-off period where you can withdraw the offer. Cooling-off periods differ from state to state in Australia.

- *Expression of interest* (EOI) – where interested buyers submit their best offers in writing for the property by a specific date to the real estate agent.

No matter what the method of sale is, this is where your hard work and negotiation skills will pay off. You need to know what your budget limit is and stick with it. Making sure your due diligence is in order is key before making an offer. This includes things like doing market research to look at comparable properties, contract review, review of owners' corporation/strata report (if applicable) and building and pest inspection, which would highlight any building defects or problems. This is to make sure the property is worth the offer you are planning to put forward.

Due diligence means checking every aspect of a property to make sure it's the right fit for what you are looking for and it's worth the money you are paying.

If it's an auction, your due diligence needs to be completed beforehand as the sale is final. You may even consider making a pre-auction offer to avoid the property going to auction at all.

If you are attending the auction yourself, don't forget to bring your driver's license to register on auction day and have your finances ready. There is no shortage of bidding strategies and tactics to consider. Some advise to bid early to assert dominance; others recommend staying silent until the bidding slows down towards the end. Some swear by dressing casually so bidders will underestimate you; others opt to dress to the nines to project the air of confidence. What works for one may not work for another. Do your own research and determine what is the best approach to suit your circumstances and preferences for that particular auction.

What is essential is making sure you have a 'walk away price'. It can be easy to get swept up in the moment. You don't want to end up over-committing and exceeding your budget in the heat of the bidding war.

If it's a private treaty or EOI, make sure your offer is fair and reasonable. You should only put in a low-ball offer if the agent is willing to negotiate. What's fair and reasonable? You probably have an idea already from all the inspections and conversations with the sales agent. Also, don't forget to look at recent sale history for comparable sales of what similar properties sold for in the area. Depending on how 'hot' the market is, sometimes pricing from six months ago is completely out of date. A good buyer agent can definitely help to guide you too.

You may have the option to adjust your terms and put in specific conditions with your offer, such as a subject to finance or building and pest clause. Don't forget to ask your conveyancer for help with this. However, an offer subject to terms and cooling-off period will be less attractive to the seller, so do weigh up the benefits.

This is where your awesome negotiation tactics will help you get the best deal, because the highest price may not always get the property. From your conversations with the agent, do you know what the motivation of the seller is? Why are they looking to sell? Maybe they are building a new house and the house is taking longer than expected, so they want a long settlement period. Perhaps you discover something in the building and pest inspection report that you can use to negotiate the pricing on. Knowing all the facts will help you put in a reasonable offer suited to both your and the seller's needs.

As a matter of best practice, it's wise to put your offer in writing. The agent is obligated to pass on your offer to the seller and initiate the process. You might need to pay a holding deposit during this time to show that you're committed. Remember to keep your broker and conveyancer updated so they can act quickly when needed.

Once your offer has been accepted

Once the seller accepts your offer, you will exchange contracts with the seller and transfer the deposit, which is usually around 5–10%. There is usually a cooling-off period (except for an auction). You can cancel the contract during this time, but you may lose your deposit. Cooling-off rules vary from state to state, for example: it is five business days in New South Wales and a 0.28% forfeit fee, while in Victoria, it's three business days and a 0.20% fee.

During this time:

- Your broker is going to be busy working with your lender to get financial approval for your purchase.
- Your conveyancer is doing legal checks such as title searches and rates, discharge of mortgage on vendor's title ... basically a lot of legal matters to make sure you fulfil your legal responsi-

bilities and your rights are protected. They will be working with your broker to make sure the property is transferred to you. They liaise on your behalf with the seller for all matters concerning the purchase.

- You will have gone through the building and pest report and have a good understanding whether there are any defects or problems.

This is an exciting and nerve-racking time. The experts around you should be keeping you updated and providing guidance on what you need to do.

The mortgage

Prior to settlement, your broker will help you to finalise your mortgage options. The mortgage contract is usually around 30 years. As part of this contract, you commit to paying the loan back to the lender (+ interest), and the property is offered as collateral to the lender.

You may hear quite a few terms being thrown around, such as principle, interest only, fixed rate, variable rate, offset, redraw. What are they and what's the difference?

Understanding these terms and structuring your loan in the right way can save you a lot of money in the long run.

Loan types

Principal and interest loan – your payments cover both the loan amount and the interest. This can be good for paying down your loan faster.

Interest only loan – your payment only covers the interest on the loan. This is often popular with some property investors to keep their running costs down.

Quick tip

If you choose fortnightly repayments instead of monthly, you are essentially making one additional monthly payment in a year. This can help to reduce the life of the loan and lower the total loan amount you have to pay.

Rate types

Fixed rate – the interest rate remains the same for the duration of the fixed period. This can be helpful for budgeting as your repayments do not change for the fixed period.

Variable rate – the interest rate might change at any time. This offers more flexibility, and you can make additional repayments and benefit from any interest rate decreases.

Account types

Offset account – this is a transaction account linked to your loan, typically available with a variable rate loan. Money sitting in your offset account 'offsets' the total you owe on the loan. For example: your home loan has a balance of $500,000, and you have $50,000 in the offset account linked to the loan; the bank charges you interest on the balance, which is $500,000 – $50,000 = $450,000. You will pay less interest over time compared to not having the offset account. This can be a good way to reduce interest if you have a bit of money set aside.

Redraw account – this is a feature attached to your loan where the money in your redraw facility counts against the balance of your loan to reduce the interest you pay. You can access the extra payments you've made if needed.

Don't forget you have the option to split your loan too. For example, you may have 50% of your loan under a fixed rate and 50% on a variable rate with an offset account.

Settlement

The end is in sight: you are on the home stretch and the place is nearly yours! The typical settlement period is about four to six weeks. Your team will be busy dotting the I's and crossing the T's behind the scenes to make sure settlement happens on the agreed date.

You need to make sure you have the money ready to complete the sale, such as stamp duty, legal fees, insurances etc. Don't forget to arrange a final inspection in the week before settlement. This is to make sure the house is in the same condition and has all the inclusions per the contract as when it was sold to you.

Your conveyancer will get the settlement statement ready and attend the settlement. Once all the documents and money are exchanged between your lender and the seller's representative, your conveyancer will give you the good news that you are now a property owner. The real estate agent will be in touch to handover the keys.

Don't forget to start the process to make sure all the rates, bills, etc have been signed over to your name. You are now officially a homeowner!

Investment property tips

For those of you who are interested in investing in property, it is a long-term game like other investment types with fluctuations with pricing and interest rates. Entering the property market comes with a higher barrier to entry with the high upfront cost. No wonder only 20% of Australian tax payers own an investment property. To join this group and expand your investment portfolio, I would like to share some of the personal lessons I've learnt along the way.

- Be clear with your property investment goals because these goals will provide you with clear direction on the property you will buy. In other words, buy with the end in mind. For example, if your goal is having additional regular income, you might look at properties that are generating a positive return. If you want to target long-term wealth accumulation, you might look at properties in areas that are likely to have strong capital growth. Or you might look for the dream investment property that has both. This will help guide you to make the right choices in line with your overarching financial goals.

- Cast your geographical net wider than your backyard. If you don't have a high-paying job or have access to financial support like the Bank of Mum and Dad, it can be difficult to get your foot on the ladder, especially in metro cities like Sydney or Melbourne where $1 million dollars probably won't stretch to an inner-city detached house with a garden. You may want to consider another city or a regional centre instead of focusing on properties within a 30-minute radius of where you live.

- Don't fall in love with the house – location is always king. Location always does the heavy lifting for increase in value over time. This makes sense, right? Because you can renovate your property to be the most amazing house you will ever see, but you can't change its location.

- Don't buy a property to minimise your tax. Make investment decisions to make money, not just to pay less tax. While the goal isn't to purchase just for tax benefits, you still shouldn't pay any more tax than necessary. Just like running a business, you need to make sure you have a good handle on your income and outgoings, keep good records, and have a good understanding of what you can and can't claim.

- Talk to a quantity surveyor to check whether getting a depreciation schedule would be worthwhile for your property. This is an extensive report that allows you to claim deductions for the natural wear and tear on the fittings, fixtures and building structure of your property. This means you can claim tax deductions to lower your taxable income.

- Know your capabilities and limits. If you don't like DIY and you are too busy to manage tradespeople, it might not be wise to buy a house that requires extensive renovations. You want property investment to be a positive experience and not cause unnecessary stress. If investing is enjoyable, then you're more likely to be in it for the long haul.
- Don't just buy the property under your personal name. There are other structures that are worth investigating, such as trusts, companies and self-managed super funds. Speak to an accountant to discuss what the best ownership structure for purchasing the property under is, as this will impact on your borrowing capacity and tax implications. In fact, don't forget to have a chat with your accountant to discuss your investment plans before making any commitments.
- Have a great property manager. A good property manager should have solid local area knowledge, good credentials and reviews, and a thorough understanding of tenancy legislations. They can help you with the day-to-day – liaising with tenants, organising repairs, collecting rent on time, and making sure the rent is at market rate. They can also help guide you through the big stuff – such as tenants breaking their lease early or causing damage. If you want to self-manage, it could still be a good idea to have a property manager do the initial parts like advertising, property showings and tenancy checks.
- Spend the time doing due diligence to make sure the property is the right fit and worth the money you are going to pay. Dive a bit deeper to make an informed decision:
  - » Research the people who live in the area – are they singles, young families or retirees? What kinds of properties would they like to live in? This will give you an idea of the ideal property for the area. If the area is full of retirees in

their seventies, and the property you are interested in is a double-storey, six-bedroom house, it's probably not the right fit for the typical demographic for the area.

- What's their average income? Ideally, up to 30% of their income would service the rent. Anything higher than this increases the chance of rental stress, which could lead to tenant turnover.
- Consider the amount of owner-occupiers vs. renters. It is likely to be the owner-occupiers that drive up prices rather than investors when it comes to re-sale value, because they are likely to be more emotional buyers.
- Think about the area characteristics – what is the local infrastructure and transportation like? Is there good government spending for the area? Is there more than one industry in the region? Does the property sit in a flood zone or bush-fire zone? Is there a lot of development happening?
- What's the vacancy rate? This is the percentage of rental properties that are untenanted and available for rent at that point in time. A healthy rate is usually around 2–3%. When the number is below this, there is a high rental demand. A higher percentage indicates there are more properties than demand. This is going to give you an idea of how popular your property will be as a rental at that time.
- What's the rental yield? This is the amount of rental income you can expect from your property. It's typically low in capital cities because the price to purchase is high. A higher yield can mean better cash flow and better return on investment.
- It's calculated as = (weekly rent x 52 / purchase price) x 100

This number can vary greatly depending on many factors, such as type of property, location, vacancy rate and overall market conditions.

» Keep an eye on your investment – such as your home loan and house equity. The equity is likely to grow over time (hopefully!). If there are things you can do to grow the value of the property, such as renovation, and the lender re-values your property to a higher amount, that means you have also grown your equity.

I personally love property as an investment class. After all, everyone needs a place to sleep. No matter who you are or where you're from, everyone deserves a roof over their head. This also means a constant demand for places to live.

Another reason is leverage. Instead of using only your own money, you are also borrowing a proportion of the property's value from a lender to buy the property. When the property's value goes up, the increase is not only on your contribution but the entire value of the property. Even a small increase in value can mean a big gain for you.

Picture this: you earn $100,000 per year. Because you are awesome, you got a 10% pay rise at work. Now you are on $110,000. That's a pretty good increase, right? Suppose you also own a property worth $500,000 and the real estate market is growing. The value of the property goes up by 10% – now the house is valued at $550,000.

This is the magical part. That 10% raise at work added $10,000 to your salary, which is great. Yet that very same 10% increase in property value increased the worth by $50,000. Think what you can do with this leverage. The great thing is that you didn't have to do much, apart from owning that property. That is – that's pretty wild!

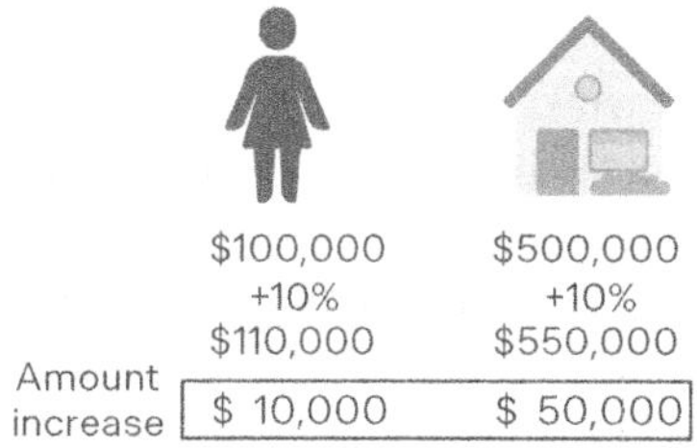

Commercial property

The information we have covered so far applies only to residential properties. Residential is usually much more talked about, and there is a lot of data and information available, but we don't want to forget about commercial properties. Commercial properties are used for business purposes – retail, industrial, office space, hotels, medical facilities, cafes and restaurants, etc.

Other than the intended use of the property, there are some big differences between residential property and commercial property to be aware of if you are considering purchasing the latter.

The good stuff	The not-so-good stuff
• More income for you. Tenants are usually responsible for the expenses for a commercial property, such as taxes, rates and insurance, whereas the landlord tends to be responsible for these expenses for a residential. • Longer lease. A commercial lease term may span a few years, typically longer than a residential one, as businesses need stability to establish themselves. • Less responsibilities. Tenants generally tend to take on more responsibilities for repairs and maintenance (lease dependent). • Control and customisation. The lease is dependent on the contract between you and the tenant and not subject to residential legislations.	• Higher deposit and higher interest rates. Most of the financial lenders will loan you up to 70% of the property value, so you need around 30% deposit. Interest rates tend to be higher than a residential property loan. • Longer vacancies. Vacancies tend to be longer than residential because finding the right business, lease negotiation and customisation can be complex. • The lease is more complex, so a solicitor should be engaged to make sure of its legality and accuracy. • Due diligence can be more difficult compared to residential. Information such as comparable pricing and resources is harder to find.

Commercial properties can be a good part of your property investment journey to expand your portfolio. Due diligence is very important for residential, but it is crucial for commercial properties. Proper research and a good understanding of market dynamics are key to capitalising on the opportunities commercial properties offer.

TAKE CHARGE

What are your investment goals? Is it just to learn how shares work? Do you want to generate enough income from your investments and live off the income?

What kind of investment appeals to you? Jump online and start doing some research and planning.

Have you got some smart investors around you? Why not buy them a coffee and pick their brains? Talk to someone who can help to guide you – where and how to start. Learn from their experiences.

Have you considered starting an investment club with like-minded people? Invite your family or friends for an investment evening. Each of you can research and present on different investment options.

You don't need to suffer analysis paralysis. Get an understanding of the basics and start small.them a coffee and pick their brains? Talk to someone who can help to guide you – where and how to start. Learn from their experiences.

Ninth thing – make your superannuation work for you

I sometimes feel like super is an unsung hero of the financial world for everyday Australians. Since its introduction as a mandatory requirement in 1992, it has been helping working Australians to proactively prepare for their retirement. It's like a forced savings and investment plan, so you can't get your hot little hands on it easily. The money in your super is meant to grow through investments for you to reap the benefits when you reach retirement age. Because it usually works quietly in the background, people sometimes don't pay enough attention to it. But giving it some love is well worth the time!

Picture this, you have $100 in your wallet, and someone took $11 from it. Wouldn't you want to know why and where that money is going? If you found out that someone is using the money to invest on your behalf, then wouldn't you want to know what they are investing on and how well the investments are doing?

At a glance

For most working Australians, your employer pays super into your super account. This contribution is on top of your regular wage/salary. At the time of writing, your employer must pay 11% of your gross income to your super fund. You can also make voluntary contributions towards your super fund yourself.

Your super fund is governed by a trustee and the appointed investment managers invest money on your behalf. They invest your money into different investment products like bonds, stocks, property, etc. – with the aim of increasing your money over time. They are obliged to carefully manage your money so it will increase steadily until your retirement.

Once you retire or reach 'preservation age', you will be able to access your super. However, there are circumstances where you can access your super earlier.

Preservation age is the age where you can acess your superannuation.

Date of birth	Preservation age
1 July 1962 – 30 June 1963	58
1 July 1963 – 30 June 1964	59
From July 1964	58

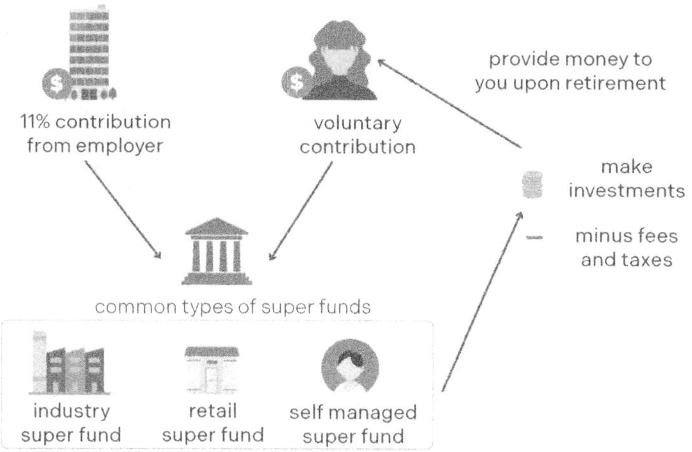

Why super matters

If you are curious to know how your balance compares to others in your age group, here's the average balance for different age groups for working females and males in Australia.

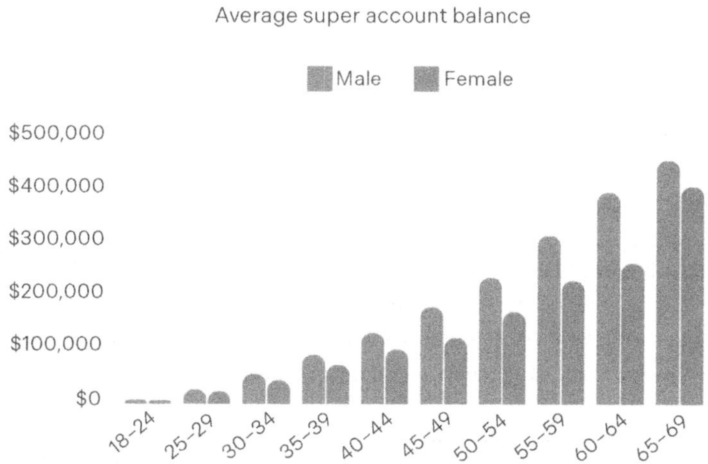

Figure 7: *average super balance by age and sex, source - ASFA, 2023.*

Super is not just another deduction from your pay. It is a safety net to make sure you can have a comfortable and enjoyable retirement when the time comes. Because quite a healthy chunk of your income goes into your super, it naturally plays a big role when it comes to your finances.

The amount of money each of us needs for a comfortable retirement will be different. According to the Association of Superannuation Funds of Australia (ASFA), if you are around retirement age and own your home, having about $545,000 in your super account for singles or $640,000 for couples is the target to enjoy a comfortable retirement lifestyle.

Unfortunately, many Australians will not reach this number, and this is particularly noticeable among women. Just over 35% of women feel confident they are likely or definitely will have enough money for retirement, while 65% of men do. Just look at the graph to see the balance difference.

We have already touched on the fact that women tend to live longer and earn less. Women often have more career breaks, taking time off to have children and taking care of family. This means we miss out on income during those breaks. It is also likely to affect our earning potential, which means less income. Since super contributions are usually 11% of the gross income, this means less money saved for retirement.

In the following sections, we will explore super in more detail to help you bridge the gap.

Getting super smart

The more you investigate different aspects of super, the better informed your decisions will be. Remember the power of compounding? Every 1% makes a big difference, especially when it comes to retirement planning since we usually can't touch it for quite a few years to come.

A fantastic thing about investment earnings in your super is that they only get taxed at 15%. This is usually much lower than your standard tax rate, which means you can keep more of your profit compared to investing outside super, where the higher tax rates can eat into your returns.

Different funds

There are a lot of super funds out there and they can be categorised into 5 main types:

Industry funds	Retail funds	Self-managed super funds (SMSF)	Public sector funds	Corporate funds
These are profit-for-member funds, so the members share the profit and not the shareholders. You may have heard some of the names such as AwareSuper, AustralianSuper and HostPlus. They typically have lower fees but more limited investment options.	These are usually owned and run by banks and financial institutions, such as; AMP and BT superannuation. These are for profit so they target to keep some of the returns they make to their shareholders. Retail funds fees are usually higher than those of industry funds, but have a more comprehensive range of investment options.	These are private super funds that people manage themselves. You have a lot more autonomy over the investment decisions and have to stick to the same mandated rules as a super fund. This is appealing for those who want more investment control and are willing to invest the time and effort to manage their own super.	These are for government workers, who often receive higher super contributions than your average worker.	These are typically set up by some of the biggest companies, e.g. Telstra, for their employees.

Different investment options

Apart from different super funds, there are also different investment options available within the super funds. Most allow you to choose between pre-mixed options and some more specialty options. Research shows about 80% of Australians with super have their money invested in a default option chosen by their employer or based on industry standards. Within this group, 20% actively chose this option, and the remaining didn't make a selection at all.

While you don't need to make specific investment choices, a good premixed option may be all you need for most people. No matter what, it's still wise to take an interest in aligning your investment strategy for your super. After all, it's your super money!

Premixed

Premixed option is like a set menu at a restaurant. It includes a good mix of different assets selected by investment managers. The mix is usually categorised based on their potential growth and associated risks. The mix and exact offering would be different from super fund to super fund. Here are some common premix categories:

High growth	Growth	Balanced	Conservative
Maximum capital growth. Mainly invest in growth assets, such as shares, the higher potential for growth comes with higher risk	Targeting higher returns over the long term. Mainly invest in growth assets for capital growth over the long term	Balance between growth and risk. Focus on a diversified mix of investment assets. Targeting moderate growth over the long term	Prioritises stability. Mainly invest in cash and fixed income investments. Targeting stable returns.

Many many more...

Some super funds allow you to have greater control. If you don't want to go with a set menu, then you might be able to mix it up a little with items from the à la carte menu with different asset types. There are single asset class options: international shares, Australian shares, property, fixed interest, cash, etc. There are even some specialised ones like sustainable/ethical investments and sector specific investments.

If you want total control over your investment choices, comfortable with your financial knowledge and willing to dedicate the time to look after your own super, then you might consider becoming one of the 1.1 million Australians that is a member of their self-managed super fund. Be careful, it's not for the faint hearted.

Contributions

For your super balance to grow in your fund, you've got to have money in it to start with. I'm going to say it again, but remember compounding? Small dollars now make a huge difference later!

There are several ways you can contribute towards your super.

From your employer

If you are an employee, your employer is legally obligated to pay 11% of your gross salary to your super fund. This super guarantee is going to increase again in 2024. If you are flying solo as self-employed, there is no obligation for you to make mandatory contributions. While it's not mandatory, why not consider it, given the many benefits it brings.

From you

There are a couple of options for you to give your super balance a boost:

- Before tax (**concessional**) contribution. You can do this through salary sacrifice, where you can ask your employer to pay part of your gross salary into your super fund, or you can make the payment directly to the fund and make a claim. Since these contributions are taxed at 15%, it has the added benefit of you paying less tax.
- After tax (**non-concessional**) contributions. You may be able to claim a tax deduction for this one too, but you have to inform your super fund and be eligible.

There are limits to how much for concessional and non-concessional contributions you can make. We will touch on that soon.

From your spouse

If you are not working because you're taking care of family, or if you earn less money than your spouse, then your spouse can pitch in and make contributions towards your super fund. There are two ways your spouse can do this:

Directly into your super as a non-concessional contribution. If you earn less than $37,000 and your spouse contributes $3,000 to your super, then your spouse can claim a tax offset of $540. Your spouse can contribute more, but the non-concessional cap applies and the tax offset is maxed out at $540.

- Concessional contributions splitting. Your spouse can split up to 85% of the concessional contributions they already made into their own super and roll them over to your super.

There are some eligibility criteria to meet, so do check the ATO's website for specific details.

From the government

If you are a low- or moderate-income earner, the government chips in with extra support to help with your super:

- Low-income super tax offset (LISTO). If you earn less than $37,000 a year, you could qualify for a payment up to $500.
- Co-contribution scheme. If you earn less than $57,016, the government will contribute up to 50c for every $1 you pay into your super, to a maximum of $500.

If you're eligible, then the government will work out the exact amount when you lodge a tax return and pay it directly to your super fund automatically.

From your home

If you are 55 years and older and have owned your home for more than 10 years, you can add $300,000 (or $600,000 per couple) from the sale of the home into your super. And it's tax-free! There are some extra eligibility criteria too, so double check the ATO's website for the latest information.

So how much can you contribute to your super?

In 2024, you can contribute a maximum of $30,000 (instead of the previous $27,500) towards your super as concessional (pre-tax) per financial year. This amount is taxed at only 15%. If you go over this amount, then the extra amount will be taxed at your usual individual tax rate. So ≤ $30,000 taxed at 15%, ≥ $30,000 taxed at usual marginal tax rate.

If there's less than $500,000 in your super on 30 June, and you didn't put the maximum amount in, then you can 'carry forward' that unused allowance and add it to this year's cap, up to five years. For example, if your concessional contribution was $10,000 last year, then you can carry forward the $17,500 to this year, which means your limit will be $45,000.

There is also the non-concessional (after tax) contribution limit of $120,000 (previously $110,000). You will be able to contribute more than this if you qualify for the 'bring forward' rule. You can 'bring forward' contributions from future years if you are under 75 and your super balance is less than $1.9 million.

One question I often hear is 'should I put money into super or use that money to invest outside super?'

Well it depends...

- Investing outside super gives you more control over your investment choices.
- Concessional tax rate is only at 15%, compared to your individual tax rate (likely a lot higher than 15%). This is a real tax advantage.
- You can't access your super until you retire/ preservation age. How does that align with your financial goals?

Insurances in your super

Your super doesn't just cover your retirement, there is the added advantage of insurance coverage in your super. We briefly covered the insurances that are available within your super fund under the chapter on insurance. They are *life* insurance, *total permanent disability* insurance and *income protection* insurance (this one is not always automatic).

You automatically get given the default cover when you join a super fund. There's no need to share your medical history or do any health exams. There are some exceptions to this automatic enrolment rule, such as if you are either under 25 or over 65, or if your insurance is under $6000.

The default cover usually depends on your age and occupation. The insurance from different funds can be quite different – the coverage, premiums paid and actual terms. Most Australians don't pay much attention to these insurances and just stick with the default coverage, so it's best to take a look to check the details to know what you are entitled to. There's the option to apply for additional coverage if the default insurance doesn't quite meet your needs. If you happen to have a self-managed super fund (SMSF), then you can choose your own insurance and insurance provider.

Insurances through super usually end around the age of 65 to 70. This is a bit different to insurances outside super, when your cover usually stays as long as you keep paying the premiums.

Beneficiary options

Did you know that your super account isn't directly owned by you? It's held in a trust by the super fund's trustee. To make sure your super and any insurance you have in your super go to the people you want, you need to nominate beneficiaries. This should also form part of your estate planning process.

A beneficiary is anyone that receives money from your super fund when you pass away. This could be:

- Your children
- Your spouse or partner
- Anyone you share a close relationship with
- Anyone that relies on you financially
- Your estate or executor (the person you chose to handle your affairs).

There are three types of beneficiary nominations:

- *Binding* beneficiary nomination. When you make a binding nomination, it's basically you giving a legal order to your super's trustee. They are legally obligated to follow your instructions and pay the money exactly. There can be a time limit associated with binding nominations, so you are responsible to keep it up to date.

- *Non-binding* beneficiary nomination. When the nomination is non-binding, it's like you saying this is a preference, rather than strict instructions. It is the super's trustee that will have the final say. They will carefully consider factors such as who your dependents are and other relevant information before making a decision on where your benefits would go.
- *Reversionary* beneficiary nomination. This nomination is specific and applies to the income from a pension within your super. If you nominate a reversionary beneficiary, that means the income from your pension automatically goes to that person when you pass away.

If you did not make a nomination, then the super's trustee will use their discretion to decide who to pay the benefit to.

Accessing your super

So you have been working hard and contributing towards your super, but when can you actually access this pool of money? It's meant for you when you retire, which involves you stopping working and having no intentions to return to the workforce. There are other circumstances where you can also access it:

- When you reach preservation age. For most Australians, you can access your super when you reach preservation age; this age varies depending on when you are born. The table on page 148 shows this in more detail.
- If you are unable to work again due to a medical condition or terminal illness.

- Compassionate grounds. For expenses such as funerals, medical treatments or home modifications if you have no other way to pay for these.
- Financial hardship. If you can't meet your living expenses and have been receiving government benefits for 26 weeks.
- Departing Australia Superannuation Payment. If you were in Australian on a temporary visa and are leaving permanently.
- If you are buying your first home through First Home Super Saver (FHSS) scheme. You can voluntarily contribute up to $15,000 per year, to a maximum of $50,000 across all years. When you are ready to buy or build your first home, you can apply to the ATO to release your eligible contributions, along with associated earnings for the purchase. There are some financial benefits:
    - Super contributions taxed at concessional rate of only 15%
    - When you withdraw your eligible contributions, the taxable part is subject to your individual tax rate but with a 30% tax offset, i.e. a 30% discount.

As you can see, there are many circumstances where you may be able to access your super early. Each of these do have specific conditions you must meet. There can be tax implications associated with some of these early releases; make sure you check with the ATO for the latest information. Super can act like a lifeline and provide financial support when you need it the most. What an unsung hero super is!

Keep an eye on your super

It's a good idea to check your super balance regularly, the rule of thumb is once every 3 months. How else would you know your employer is putting the right amount in there? Hopefully, you're not one of the 33% of Australians that check their super less than this, or the 10% that never check their balance.

How many super funds do you have?

One in four of us have two or more super accounts. How does this happen? Well, you may have changed jobs and just started with the super fund recommended by your new employer. Over time, these multiple accounts can add up and you may forget about these funds. In fact, they add up to $16 billion dollars.

That's $16 billion dollars in lost and unclaimed super and a bunch of forgotten money sitting with the ATO.

The whole point of super is to make sure you have this pool of money for your golden years. When you have multiple accounts, each will have its own set of fees. The fees slowly nibble away at your balance. They may seem small, but they do add up over time, especially when you have multiple accounts. By consolidating your super, you can save money by paying one set of fees and making it easier for yourself to keep track of your super.

Visit ato.gov.au/checkyoursuper to learn more about managing and accessing information about your super, including details on unclaimed or lost super funds.

How do you choose?

Choosing the right super fund and investment option is a weighty financial decision for your retirement. Over half of Australians let their employer choose what fund they end up in, and even more on the default investment option, like we discussed earlier, without further investigation.

So you probably shouldn't leave it to chance! Why not consider taking an active role in managing your retirement fund – explore different options and make the best choice for you?

There are quite a few factors to consider: check investment options to see how they match your goals and risk appetite, associated fees, insurance premiums and coverage, membership benefits and past performance (although past performance does not equate to future performance).

The ATO's website has a useful resource – the YourSuper comparison tool, which looks at different funds and their performances. This will be helpful for comparing the options available.

TAKE CHARGE

If you haven't reviewed your super balance for a while, then it's high time. You are investing 11% of your salary, so make this 11% count.

If you are currently on the default option, then check to see if this option is right for you. Are you happy with the returns and fees? If not, then start doing research on what you could change it to – whether it's another option at the same super fund, or another super fund entirely.

Are your beneficiaries up to date? Make sure you put some nominations in place.

Are you making extra contributions towards your super? Does this make sense for you?

Tenth thing – a successful woman thrives with a winning team

To be financially smart and to achieve successes in life, we can't do it alone.

Take a world-class athlete, for example: they follow strict training regimes, eat nutritious foods and look after their mental and physical wellbeing. They have coaches who provide guidance and help to refine their techniques, performance and offer support. They have physicians who provide top level medical care, check out any injuries and monitor their general health. They have psychologists who work on their mental state to help them stay motivated and focused. They have nutritionists who create diet plans that optimise recovery, energy levels and health.

It takes a village. It's all about giving the athlete the best possible chance at succeeding.

The same goes for your financial journey.

Start with yourself

You are the star athlete of your financial journey.

In a 2023 study conducted by ANZ, it was highlighted that women felt less confident and secure about their financial future than their male counterparts in almost all age groups. To counter this, having the right knowledge and cultivating the right mindset is key.

Take accountability to make sure you have the right knowledge and mindset and spend time educating yourself about financial things. Start with the basics like budgeting and managing debt, and keep on stepping up your skillset with investing. There is no shortage of material out there – books, podcasts, seminars, online searches ... This knowledge is going to help you make more informed and better decisions with your finances.

Embrace growth mindset. A growth mindset encourages continuous learning and putting your learning to use. Your life is always changing. The changes in your circumstances mean you always need to be on the look out to make sure you are making the best of your financial situation. Sometimes you will make mistakes and that's okay. Learn from them and use them as stepping stones for improving your financial literacy.

Be tough but patient with yourself. It's a marathon, not a sprint. Develop the discipline to stick to your financial goals and don't go off-track. But if you do, be kind. Reflect and get back on the wagon as soon as possible. Just like the athlete pushing themselves during training, you can challenge yourself to make consistent progress that aligns with your goals. Discipline is like a muscle that grows stronger with practice; it will become a habit that becomes easier to maintain over time.

Only you have the power and control over your actions. Life has a tendency to throw curve balls at you when you are least expecting it. The winners pick themselves back up, assess the new situation and keep on going.

Your life partner

If you happen to have a spouse or partner, it's likely you have to combine your money in some way. I don't know about you, but it was a scary thing when I had to do it. It's one thing to be responsible for my own livelihood, but quite another when you combine your life with someone else. This is not to mention our differing money personalities and views on spending habits.

Money is the number one thing that most couples argue about. Given that nearly half of marriages end in divorce, it's likely that money and finances play a rather contentious role. Given how important it is, let's shine a light on it. Why do we not talk about money when we first date someone? Just as you ask questions about their careers or families, weave some questions into your early conversations so you can understand their attitude towards finances and their financial goals. You might even have them as the top 10 questions you ask during your dates!

Do you have any siblings? What do you do for work? How do you feel about money and what are you like with it? What are your financial goals over the next five or 10 years?

Attitude towards money is often deep-rooted. If you have very different views and don't talk about it, then it's just asking for trouble. Open and honest communication is key. It's often difficult when you have very different opinions on what's important and what's not. If you stand on your side of the fence and don't compromise, you will never see where they are coming from and why they feel that way.

If you and your partner are committed to a long-term relationship, you can't be on this financial journey alone. You will have to support each other along the way and be each other's cheerleaders. How do your financial goals and habits look compared to theirs? What are your combined financial goals? What can each of you contribute – in time, resources and money? If you are both new on this financial journey, can you educate yourselves with the information you are interested in and teach the other person? Work to your strengths and be in charge of the things you are good at. If one of you loves numbers, maybe it makes more sense for that person to control your budget. If one of you loves research and getting to the bottom of things, perhaps that person takes the lead in conversations with a financial planner.

If you are not working with each other, it can feel like you are working against each other. It just doesn't work if one person wants to save for a house and the other prioritises spending money on the latest gadgets.

Your network circle

I once heard that you're the average of the five people you spend the most time with. When you are spending time with people, they are guiding the conversational topics you talk about. They can influence how you think and act.

It is easier to be a go-getter when you are surrounded by driven and happy individuals, and it's difficult to reach your full potential if you are always around negative people. If you hang out with people who love talking about their investment strategies, it's hard not to get swept up and think about your own.

> 'Your inner circle can influence as much as 95% of your success or failure in life.'
>
> Research by Dr McClelland, social psychologist from Harvard

Conversations reveal your mindset and experiences. If your circle can open your eyes to new perspectives and possibilities, then power to you! We are social creatures and naturally seek to fit in. We tend to adopt the behaviours, beliefs and attitudes of those around us. By being with people who have the right mindset and experiences that align with your goals, you naturally create a positive environment where you can grow and support each other.

Your social circle matters. Be intentional with the company you keep.

Your team of experts

If your toilet is blocked, you call a plumber. If you want to get better at playing tennis, you get a coach. If you want to be a world-class athlete, you need a village of experts.

Since you are the star performer of your future, surround yourself with experts who enhance and elevate your performance to reach your financial goals. Your experts know things you don't, save you time and have resources you might not have access to. Pick and choose the ones that make sense for you. We have already talked about some of the experts you could engage for buying real estate, so make sure you go back and revisit those pages.

- Accountant

  They can provide financial planning advice (some of them), identify deductions for tax, and give guidance on structure and setup, while making sure you are compliant with the necessary tax regulations. They can help you to optimise your financial journey and make informed decisions about investments with personalised tax advice. Some specialise in specific areas, such as small businesses or property investment.

Many accountants are members of professional bodies such as CPA Australia and Chartered Accountants Australia and New Zealand. If you have an accountant filing tax returns on your behalf, make sure they are registered with the Tax Practitioners Board.

- Estate lawyer

  They can help with your estate planning and provide guidance for complex family/business structures. They draft and implement documents like wills and trusts, and devise strategies for asset distribution to beneficiaries. They assist you with establishing powers of attorney and health directives, making sure your financial and personal decisions are honoured, not to mention educate you on the process and laws that will affect your estate.

- Financial advisor

  They can help you conduct a financial health check and work with you to convert your goals into actionable plans. They should help you understand what will be involved in meeting these goals – budgeting, savings, investment plan, insurances. They can help you make investment decisions like optimising super contributions, etc.

  Financial advisors should have an Australian Financial Services (AFS) license and can be found on the Financial Advisers Register. This is a public database that the Australian Securities & Investment Commission (ASIC) maintains to help you find out more information about the advisor and verify the advisor is qualified.

- Financial coach

  They can help you build good money behaviour and stay on track with your goals. They offer guidance on how you can handle money better and make smart financial choices.

   » While there are no formal qualifications required, many coaches have qualifications in finance, accounting or related fields.

- Mortgage broker

  They can help you secure financing for property purchases. They will guide you through different options from different lenders, interest rates available and loan structures.

  Brokers should be members of industry associations such as the Finance Brokers Association of Australia (FBAA) or Mortgage & Finance Association of Australia (MFAA). They must have an Australian Credit License (ACL), which is given by ASIC.

As with any profession, there are good ones and not-so-good ones. You really have to do your research and, hopefully, you don't have to kiss too many frogs before you find the right ones for you. Some recommendations for you to consider:

- Ensure they have the right credentials, right experience and a great track record for what they are practising in. Do they have the right qualifications for what they are practising? Do they belong to the right professional organisation? (Often these organisations hold their members to a code of ethics and require continuing professional development.) Does their experience suit you and your specific needs? How is their track record with helping people like you? You want to make sure they know what they are doing and they have the expertise and experience you are after.

- Seek recommendations from family and friends. If you have a family member or friend you trust around financial matters, ask for their recommendations of great professionals. You can't beat word-of-mouth, but still consider whether it's the right fit for you – for example, continuing to use the accountant that your parents have been using when you may have outgrown their services.

- Ask them questions around your specific situation. This is going to help you determine whether they are helping you and not pushing their own agenda. Are they recommending a product to you because it's the right fit for you to achieve your goals, or is it because they are getting some sort of incentive?
- Talk to a few and don't just go with the first one you talk to. This helps you compare their approach, expertise and how they fit your needs.
- Do you like them? If you don't like them, or something doesn't feel right, reconsider. You will be dealing with them a lot, so if you don't like them, it's not going to work. Trust your gut.
- Consider their responsiveness. You want to deal with someone who responds to your queries and offers you advice in a timely manner. Taking days to reply to calls or messages really isn't on.
- Read the fine print of anything they put in front of you. Nobody likes to read long pages of text, but you have to understand what is being offered to make sure it's the best solution for you.

These professionals are the experts in their field; they will help to enhance your performance. They are going to help to put you on the podium, but you're still the star athlete performing!

TAKE CHARGE

It's up to you now! Make a plan and make some commitments:

First, to yourself. What information would you commit to learning? How are you going to make sure you are continuously learning? How are you implementing what you are learning?

Second, to your surroundings. Whether it's your partner or friends. How can you talk about finances and have meaningful conversations about money and achieving your financial goals?

Third, to your team of experts. Who do you need in your corner and how are you going to find them?

Last pearls of wisdom

You have made it to the end!

We have covered a lot. I hope reading this book has increased your appetite for more financial knowledge, and you have started taking action forwards your financial goals.

Before you take over the world, I would like to share some last pearls of wisdom I have learnt along the way and wish my parents had taught me.

- Let's talk about money and finances.

  Our discomfort with money and discussing it openly holds us back. Let's break down the barriers and normalise conversations about finances. Sit down with your friends, partners, family members and even your beloved pets to talk about finances. Sharing knowledge and experiences can be empowering and liberating.

- Avoid the lifestyle creep.

  As your income grows over the years, so does your disposable income. The more you have, the more you may want. If you have read *The Millionaire Next Door*, the truly wealthy value smart financial decisions over showing off their wealth. It's not about driving the latest model cars or wearing the latest designer clothing (unless they are part of your financial goals).

- Think about the opportunity cost.

  There are often trade-offs with the decisions you make. It might be money, time or effort. If you drive around for a couple of hours to hunt for the best deals in stores, perhaps you would be better off spending some of that time negotiating a better rate for your utilities. It is about being intentional with your choices and making decisions that align with what matters most to you.

- Build money confidence.

  Your future is your responsibility. It's not the responsibility of your parents, spouse/partner or anybody else around you. It's yours. Find mentors you trust and who can help you along the way. Be clear on your goals so you can create clear plans and take action in what you learn along the way. Remember to celebrate the wins, no matter how small, so you get those dopamine hits.

- We all have 24 hours in a day.

  It doesn't matter if you are rich or poor, live on an island or at the top of a tower, we all have 24 hours in a day. It's our choice of how we spend our time. Our time is finite, our potential isn't – neither is our financial future. It's never too late to make a start.

Thank you for sticking with me. I am honoured you have picked up this book and allowed me to share these 10 lessons with you. Now go forth and make a start – be the star of your financial story.

If you would like to get in touch, I would love to hear from you.

Please reach out to me at www.shecanfinance.com

Acknowledgements

There have been many people, books, podcasts and resources that have sparked my passion in this book venture and made it possible.

Here's a super short list:

To my parents for the hard work and many sacrifices they had to make.

To everyone who gave up their valuable time and helped with reading drafts and providing insights.

To David Boyle, a beacon of kindness and generosity. I would never have bought my first house in Australia without your help and guidance.

To Jeremy Iannuzzelli, thank you for being our accountant extraordinaire and reading through your love languages for all things taxes.

And finally, to the many amazing women and men in my life who have been an inspiration for this book.

References

1. International Labour Organization's (ILO) "Women and Men in the Informal Economy" 2021 report and Australian Bureau of Statistics (ABS)
2. Workplace Gender Equality Agency, https://www.wgea.gov.au/pay-and-gender/gender-pay-gap-data
3. Australian Institute of Health and Welfare (AIHW) life expectancy report, 2023
4. Workplace Gender Equality Agency, "Wome's economic security in retirement", 2017
5. EA Locke and GP Latham, "A theory of goal setting & task performance", Academy of Management Review, 1991, 16(2)
6. EA Locke and GP Latham, "Building a practically useful theory of goal setting and task motivation: A 35-year odyssey", American Psychologist, 2002, 57(9):705–717.
7. 7 M Rice, "Closing in on what motivates motivation!, Nature, 2019, 570(7759)
8. G Matthews, https://www.dominican.edu/sites/default/files/2020-02/gailmatthews-harvard-goals-researchsummary.pdf Dominican University of California, 2018
9. AMP Financial Wellness report, 2022

10. Shah et al, "Paper or plastic?: How we pay influences post-transaction connection", Journal of Consumer Research, 2016, 42(5):688–708

11. Coping with COVID-19: Rethinking Australia, 2020

12. ACOSS, "Poverty rates in OECD countries", 2021, https://povertyandinequality.acoss.org.au/poverty/poverty-rates-in-oecd-countries

13. ACOSS, "Poverty in Australia 2022: A snapshot", https://povertyandinequality.acoss.org.au/a-snapshot-of-poverty-in-australia-2022/

14. IBISWorld Credit Card Issuance in Australia, Market Size 2008–2029

15. Allied Market Research press release, Ôcredit card payments market", 2023

16. Hershfield & Bartels, "The Future Self", The Psychology of Thinking about the Future, 89–109, The Guilford Press, 2018

17. Raghubir & Srivastava, "Monopoly money: The effect of payment coupling and form on spending behavior", Journal of Experimental Psychology: Applied, 2008, 14(3), 213–225

18. Schneider et al, "Mirror, Mirror 2022: reflecting poorly", Commonwealth Fund, 2021

19. "The future of retirement: bridging the gap", HSBC, 2018

20. Macrotrends 2023, https://www.macrotrends.net/1320/nasdaq-historical-chart

21. CoreLogic research data, September 2023

Made in the USA
Monee, IL
04 November 2026

67385844R10098